Student Viewer's Guide to accompany

Sol y viento

Bill VanPatten

University of Illinois at Chicago

Michael J. Leeser

Florida State University

Gregory D. Keating

University of Illinois at Chicago

Boston   Burr Ridge, IL   Dubuque, IA   Madison, WI   New York
San Francisco   St. Louis   Bangkok   Bogotá   Caracas   Kuala Lumpur
Lisbon   London   Madrid   Mexico City   Milan   Montreal   New Delhi
Santiago   Seoul   Singapore   Sydney   Taipei   Toronto

 **Higher Education**

This is an ⨆ book.

Student Viewer's Guide to accompany
Sol y viento

Published by McGraw-Hill, an imprint of The McGraw-Hill Companies, Inc., 1221 Avenue of the Americas, New York, NY 10020. Copyright © 2005 by The McGraw-Hill Companies, Inc. All rights reserved. No part of this publication may be reproduced or distributed in any form or by any means, or stored in a database or retrieval system, without the prior written consent of The McGraw-Hill Companies, Inc., including, but not limited to, in any network or other electronic storage or transmission, or broadcast for distance learning.

This book is printed on acid-free paper.

5 6 7 8 9 0 QPD QPD 0 9 8

ISBN-13: 978-0-07-296578-0
ISBN-10: 0-07-296578-9

Editor-in-chief: *Emily G. Barrosse*
Publisher: *William R. Glass*
Senior sponsoring editor: *Christa Harris*
Director of development: *Scott Tinetti*
Development editor: *Pennie Nichols*
Executive marketing manager: *Nick Agnew*
Lead production editor: *David M. Staloch*
Lead production supervisor: *Randy Hurst*
Senior supplements producer: *Louis Swaim*
Photo research coordinator: *Nora Agbayani*
Freelance photo researcher: *Judy Mason*
Compositor: *The GTS Companies/York, PA Campus*
Typeface: *10/12 Bookman*
Printer and binder: *Quebecor World Printing, Dubuque*

Credits:
Page 10 Corbis; *p. 18* Danny Lehman/Corbis; *p. 26* Jan Butchofsky-Houser/Corbis; *p. 34* Digital Stock; *p. 50* Digital Stock; *p. 58* Keith Dannemiller/Corbis; *p. 66* Ron Kaufman/Corbis

Contents

Preface

The Student Viewer's Guide to accompany *Sol y viento* is designed to help you integrate the *Sol y viento* film as a supplement in a wide variety of courses, at beginning, intermediate, or advanced levels of instruction. By using the Student Viewer's Guide, you and your students will enjoy watching the prologue and nine regular episodes of the film more and get more out of them.

Sol y viento: The Film (I)

A successful young businessman gets orders to travel abroad to secure a land deal. Occupied with other matters and unwilling to go at first, he finally accepts the assignment and soon finds himself in Chile, a country far from his native California. Here, in this Andean nation—land of fertile valleys and soaring mountains, home to the condor, a place exotic and familiar all at once—this young man regains and embraces values he had set aside years ago. He rediscovers the importance of loyalty to family and friends and learns that a person's past is part of his or her soul. He rediscovers the meaning of community and how people and their land may share a bond as strong as that between any two people. Most importantly, he comes to understand that from love, forgiveness is possible—but it is not easily dispensed. Forgiveness must be earned.

Such is the story of the exciting new movie, *Sol y viento.* Follow Jaime "James" Talavera on his unexpected journey of self-discovery. Along the way meet Mario, the talkative personal driver who becomes Jaime's first friend in a new land. Meet Carlos, the secretive administrator of the winery who is eager to sell his family's lands—and those of others. Meet doña Isabel, the matriarch of the Sol y viento winery, and don Paco, the friend of the family who travels from Mexico to aid doña Isabel as she faces a crisis that threatens to alter an entire community's way of life. Finally, meet the high-spirited María, the young woman who captures Jaime's heart and mind. However, their mutual attraction may prove to be fleeting if Jaime does not grapple with the moral issues that confront him. As events unfold and the forces of nature conspire to draw the characters together, Jaime is forced to make the most difficult decision of his life.

Sol y viento: The Film (II)

One of the central themes examined in *Sol y viento* is the interaction between the forces of nature in the everyday lives of people. In fact, the sun (**sol**) and wind (**viento**) each play crucial roles in the film, as if they were characters themselves. Thus, "Sol y viento" is not just the name of a family winery; it displays the embodiment of elements of nature that help move the plot along.

Cast of Characters

Jaime

A successful businessman from San Francisco, California, who travels to Chile to finalize a deal with the Sol y viento winery.

María

A Chilean university professor and anthropologist who has always let her head rule over her heart.

Carlos

Proprietor and administrator of the Sol y viento winery who is working on the deal with Jaime's company.

Isabel

Carlos' ailing mother and, with her now-deceased husband, original proprietor of Sol y viento.

Paco

An old family friend of Isabel, who is called away from his native Mexico to help his friend in a time of need.

Mario

A taxi driver in Jaime's employ during his stay in Chile.

Traimaqueo
The longtime foreman of the Sol y viento winery.

Yolanda
Traimaqueo's wife and Isabel's primary caregiver.

Diego
María's student assistant at the university and at anthropological dig sites.

Who are the Mapuches?

Throughout the course of the film, *Sol y viento* touches upon the plight of the Mapuche people and their struggle to retain their ancestral lands and maintain harmony with the Earth. The Mapuches are an indigenous people whose roots are found in southern and south central Chile and date back to thousands of years before the Europeans' arrival in the Western Hemisphere. In Quechua, the language of the Mapuche, **mapu** means *land* and **che** means *people*, essentially making them "people of the land." This connection to the earth is deeply rooted in the spirit and culture of the Mapuche people.

Since the 1880s, when the nations of Chile and Argentina began to appropriate ancestral Mapuche lands, the Mapuches have strived to retain these lands and, later, to make their struggles known to the world at large. In *Sol y viento*, this struggle is shown by the attempt of outsiders to purchase Mapuche lands in order to build a large dam to flood the region and produce cheap hydroelectric power.

In her book *Mi país inventado*, the acclaimed Chilean writer Isabel Allende relates a real-life struggle that echoes this theme in the film:

> *Nuestros indios no pertenecían a una cultura espléndida, como los aztecas, mayas o incas; eran hoscos, primitivos, irascibles y poco numerosos, pero tan corajudos, que estuvieron en pie de guerra durante trescientos años, primero contra los colonizadores españoles y luego contra la república. Fueron pacificados en 1880 y no se oyó hablar mucho de ellos por más de un siglo, pero ahora los mapuches —«gente de la tierra»— han vuelto a la lucha para defender las pocas tierras que les quedan, amenazadas por la construcción de una represa en el río Bío Bío.**

---

*Our Indians didn't belong to a grand culture, like the Aztecs, Mayas, or Incas; they were gruff, primitive, irritable, and few in number, but so brave that they waged war for 300 years, first against the Spanish settlers and then against the republic. They were pacified in 1880, and for more than a century you didn't hear a lot about them. But now the Mapuches —people of the earth— have renewed their fight in order to defend the few lands they have left, threatened by the construction of a dam on the Bío Bío River.
(Isabel Allende, *Mi país inventado* [Buenos Aires: Sudamericana, 2003], 56.)

One of the Mapuche characters in the film, the **machi,** is a spiritual leader of her tribe. At the beginning of the film, we see her telling a tale to a group of adults and children. As her tale unfolds, we witness how the lives of Jaime, María, and others are intricately woven into her story and how the forces of nature conspire to bring resolution to the conflicts with which they are faced.

The figurine seen here is a representation of a protective spirit in the beliefs of the Mapuche people. This spirit also plays an important role in the film, as you will see.

The Structure of the Student Viewer's Guide

The Student Viewer's Guide is designed to facilitate and assess students' comprehension of the film and to provide additional opportunities to express themselves in Spanish. When used in conjunction with other print and multimedia materials, the *Sol y viento* film and the Student Viewer's Guide play an important part in developing student proficiency in the Spanish language and promoting a better understanding of Hispanic cultures.

Dramatic and engaging, the *Sol y viento* film serves as the centerpiece for the Student Viewer's Guide. Divided into ten "episodes," consisting of a prologue and nine segments of approximately ten minutes each, the movie is easily managed for viewing in class or can be assigned as homework. If assigned as homework, it is recommended that the Instructional Version of the film be available in the Media Center or Language Lab of your institution. (It is also available for student purchase.) In the Instructional Version of the film, students see each episode multiple times with varied accompanying on-screen activities, thus maximizing their exposure to language and greatly increasing their comprehension skills. Students may also purchase the Director's Cut, which contains the complete and uninterrupted film but no on-screen activities.

With the exception of the brief **Prólogo,** the structure of each episode is consistent in the Student Viewer's Guide, thus facilitating lesson planning and integration of the materials into the curriculum. Each episode is organized as follows:

A primera vista: These activities support a first viewing of the episode.

- **Antes de ver el episodio:** In this pre-viewing section, students complete a wide variety of activity types, such as reviewing material from previous episodes, learning and practicing unfamiliar vocabulary from the episode, and guessing what may happen in the story.

- **Después de ver el episodio:** After having watched the episode, students complete a number of comprehension activities, including the guessing of unfamiliar words or phrases in context. As a final activity in this section, a cloze passage provides a brief summary of what happened in the episode.

A segunda vista: These activities support a second viewing of the episode.

- **Antes de ver el episodio:** Upon a second viewing of the episode, students are asked to listen for specific information to help them better understand the characters and the story line.

- **Después de ver el episodio:** After having watched the episode for a second time, students work with partners or in small groups to discuss topics as suggested by the episode. Topics include describing characters and their motivation, identifying key plot lines in the story, or predicting what will happen in future episodes.

Para escribir: To end each episode, students complete a process writing activity called **Para escribir.** Through a series of pre-writing and post-writing tasks (which include peer review and editing), students explore the characters and their relationships in a much more profound way as they also improve their writing skills in Spanish.

Additional Features

Here are some additional features that are found in every episode of the Student Viewer's Guide.

- **Para pensar...** appears on every episode-opening page, along with stills from the film. Questions about the images encourage students to think about the upcoming episode.

- **Nota sobre el lenguaje** features identify a particular grammar point that students may or may not have studied. The brief explanations and examples are designed to help students with language they may hear in the episode or to help them complete the activities that correspond to the episode. Topics include:

  Episodio 1: the verb **ir**
  Episodio 2: uses of **ser** and **estar**
  Episodio 3: **gustar** and object pronouns
  Episodio 4: the preterite tense
  Episodio 5: the imperfect tense
  Episodio 6: formal and informal commands
  Episodio 7: the present subjunctive
  Episodio 8: the present and past perfect
  Episodio 9: the future tense

- *Sol y viento:* **Enfoque cultural** sections explore a cultural point illustrated in the *Sol y viento* film.

- **Detrás de la cámara** boxes provide additional information not presented in the film, such as the characters' backgrounds, motivation, personalities, and so forth.

- **Icons** highlight partner/pair or group work and writing activities that require an additional sheet of paper.

- An **Answer Key,** located at the back of the Student Viewer's Guide, provides answers to many of the activities so that students can check their work.

Using the Film with the Student Viewer's Guide

As previously stated, the *Sol y viento* film is available in two versions: 1) the Director's Cut, a complete version that is the uninterrupted, full-length feature film, and 2) an Instructional Version, which divides the story into a prologue and nine regular episodes. Except for the **Prólogo,** each episode of *Sol y viento* in the Instructional Version follows the same format:*

---

*The Instructional Version of the film also contains an **Introducción** segment. It is highly recommended that you *and* your students view this segment first in order to more fully understand how to get more use out of the *Sol y viento* program.

A primera vista:

1. Students watch and complete on-screen pre-viewing activities for a first viewing of the episode.

   - **Preparación** Scenes from the preceding or other previous episodes are used to remind students about main events in the story that will help them understand the new episode.

2. Students view the complete episode.

3. Students watch and complete on-screen post-viewing activities.

   - **¿Lo captaste?** Scenes from the episode are used in a variety of multiple-choice and true-false activities to help students verify their comprehension of the main ideas and the plot of the episode they've just watched.

   - **Lengua en contexto** This section identifies language functions and structures that are covered in the *Sol y viento* textbook. Appropriate scenes from the film are subtitled in Spanish and the targeted grammar and vocabulary are highlighted in yellow. Although tied directly to the *Sol y viento* textbook, the **Lengua en contexto** sections do provide a review of general structures and vocabulary found in most beginning Spanish textbooks. Some instructors may choose to skip this segment of the episode, depending on the correspondence between the textbook in use and the focus of the episode. Topics include:

     Episodio 1: Regular **-ar** Verbs

     Episodio 2: Verbs that End in **-go** and Stem-Changing Verbs

     Episodio 3: Saber and **conocer**

     Episodio 4: The Preterite Tense

     Episodio 5: The Imperfect Tense

     Episodio 6: The Present Perfect Tense

     Episodio 7: Pseudo-Reflexive Verbs

     Episodio 8: The Conditional Tense

     Episodio 9: The Subjunctive with Indefinite or Negative Antecedents

A segunda vista:

1. Students watch and complete on-screen pre-viewing activities for a second viewing of the episode.

   - **Lo que has visto...** Scenes from the current episode are reviewed to reinforce what students have seen. Scenes from previous episodes may also be included, depending on the focus of the plot.

2. Students view the complete episode for a second time.

3. Students watch and complete on-screen post-viewing activities.

   - **¿Qué recuerdas?** Scenes from the episode are used in activities that check student comprehension of the finer details of the episode: what the characters said, what scene or quote comes next, and so forth.

   - **Diálogos e imágenes** These sections provide viewing strategies and other tips that students can apply to help them understand the language, events, and characters in the film. Topics include:

     Episodio 1: Recognizing Cultural Differences

     Episodio 2: Understanding Body Language

     Episodio 3: Analyzing Characters

     Episodio 4: Foreshadowing

     Episodio 5: Understanding a Character's Motivation

     Episodio 6: Understanding Formal and Informal Interactions in Spanish

     Episodio 7: More on Understanding a Character's Motivation

     Episodio 8: Predicting What's Going to Happen

     Episodio 9: Integrating Natural and Supernatural Elements into a Story

Supplements

■ The **Interactive CD-ROM** to accompany *Sol y viento* is available for purchase in a multiplatform format and offers students opportunities to practice their skills in Spanish, as well as the story line and characters of the *Sol y viento* film, all in an engaging multimedia environment.

■ The Student Edition of the **Online Learning Center Website** (www.mhhe.com/solyviento) provides additional language skills practice. It also helps students bring the Spanish-speaking world into their language-learning experience through a variety of cultural resources and activities. The Instructor Edition portion of the site contains many resources to assist instructors in getting the most out of the *Sol y viento* program.

Note that some of the resources on the Online Learning Center Website contain *premium content*, which corresponds to material for use with the full *Sol y viento* program. The premium content on the site is not meant for use with this Student Viewer's Guide. However, the material that you may access free of charge on the site includes vocabulary and grammar quizzes, cultural links and activities, and other resources.

Instructors have full access to all levels of content via the Instructor Edition link on the home page of the Online Learning Center. Please contact your local McGraw-Hill sales representative for your password to the Instructor Edition, as this content is password-protected.

■ Available for purchase in either VHS or DVD format, the entire *Sol y viento* film can be viewed uninterrupted (**Director's Cut**). The **Instructional Version** of the film contains the film broken out into episodes with on-screen pre- and post-viewing activities to accompany each episode.

■ The **Picture File** contains 50 images from the film that may be used as a springboard for student discussion about the film or related topics. Please contact your local McGraw-Hill sales representative for more information about the Picture File.

About the Authors

Bill VanPatten is Professor of Spanish and Second Language Acquisition at the University of Illinois at Chicago where he is also the Director of Spanish Basic Language. His areas of research are input and input processing in second language acquisition and the effects of formal instruction on acquisitional processes. He has published widely in the fields of second language acquisition and language teaching and is a frequent conference speaker and presenter. In addition to *Sol y viento,* he is also the lead author of *¿Sabías que... ?,* Fourth Edition (2004, McGraw-Hill) and *Vistazos,* Second Edition (2006, McGraw-Hill). He is also the lead author and designer of *Destinos* and co-author with James F. Lee of *Making Communicative Language Teaching Happen,* Second Edition (2003, McGraw-Hill). He is also the author of *Input Processing and Grammar Instruction: Theory and Research* (1996, Ablex/Greenwood) and *From Input to Output: A Teacher's Guide to Second Language Acquisition* (2003, McGraw-Hill), and he is the editor of *Processing Instruction: Theory, Research, and Commentary* (2004, Erlbaum). When not engaged in academic activities, he writes fiction and performs stand-up comedy.

Michael J. Leeser is Assistant Professor of Spanish in the Department of Modern Languages and Linguistics at Florida State University, where he is also Director of the Spanish Basic Language Program. Before joining the faculty at Florida State, he taught a wide range of courses at the secondary and postsecondary levels, including courses in Spanish language and Hispanic cultures, teacher preparation courses for secondary school teachers, and graduate courses in communicative language teaching and second language acquisition. He received his Ph.D. in Spanish (Second Language Acquisition and Teacher Education) from the University of Illinois at Urbana-Champaign in 2003. His research interests include input processing during second language reading as well as second language classroom interaction. His research has appeared in journals such as *Studies in Second Language Acquisition* and *Language Teaching Research.* He also co-authored the CD-ROM, along with Bill VanPatten and Mark Overstreet, for *¿Sabías que... ?,* Fourth Edition (2004, McGraw-Hill).

Gregory D. Keating will complete his Ph.D. in Hispanic Linguistics and Second Language Acquisition at the University of Illinois at Chicago in 2005. His areas of research include Spanish sentence processing, the role instruction plays in language acquisition, and the acquisition of Spanish syntax and vocabulary. His doctoral research explores the relationship between language processing and grammatical competence in the acquisition of Spanish gender agreement. He is a frequent presenter at conferences in the United States and Mexico. He is also a recipient of several teaching awards, including one from the University of Notre Dame, where he received his M.A. in Spanish Literature. In addition to teaching and research, he has supervised many language courses and teaching assistants and has assisted in the coordination of technology-enhanced lower-division Spanish language programs.

MAR CARIBE

OCÉANO ATLÁNTICO

Maracaibo

Barranquilla

PANAMÁ

Caracas

VENEZUELA

GUYANA

Georgetown

Paramaribo

Medellín

Panamá

Río Orinoco

Cayena

Bogotá

SURINAME

GUYANA FRANCESA

Cali

COLOMBIA

Quito

Ecuador

ECUADOR

Río Amazonas

Belém

Guayaquil

Manaus

PERÚ

BRASIL

Recife

Cuzco

Lima

La Paz

Brasília

Arequipa

BOLIVIA

Sucre

PARAGUAY

Antofagasta

Rio de Janeiro

Trópico de Capricornio

Asunción

CHILE

San Miguel de Tucumán

São Paulo

La Serena

OCÉANO PACÍFICO

Córdoba

Rosario

OCÉANO ATLÁNTICO

Valparaíso

URUGUAY

Santiago

ARGENTINA

Buenos Aires

Montevideo

Concepción

Río de la Plata

Bahía Blanca

Puerto Montt

Bariloche

Chiloé

AMÉRICA DEL SUR

Islas Malvinas

0   1500 kilómetros

Estrecho de Magallanes

Punta Arenas

Tierra del Fuego

0   1000 millas

Cabo de Hornos

CORDILLERA DE LOS ANDES

Los espíritus[a]

Para pensar... [b]

In a moment you will watch the **Prólogo** to the movie *Sol y viento*. Examine the photos on this page. At this point, you may not see what they suggest about the plot and characters, but consider the following: characters often represent groups of people. What types of people are represented by each person you see in the photos? Can you imagine any kind of conflict that could develop among them?

 The Interactive CD-ROM to accompany *Sol y viento* contains additional practice with the story of the film and will help you improve your skills in Spanish.

 The *Sol y viento* Online Learning Center Website contains additional practice materials. Log on to **www.mhhe.com/solyviento**.

[a]Los... *Spirits*   [b]Para... *Something to think about . . .*

SOL Y VIENTO

Antes de ver[a] el episodio

[a]Antes... *Before watching*

You are about to watch the prologue of *Sol y viento*. In this brief episode, you will meet several principal characters, and a major plot line will be established. Before watching the episode, complete the activities in **Antes de ver el episodio.**

Actividad A   En grupos

In groups of three, discuss the following questions. You may use English at this time.

1. What do the words **sol** and **viento** mean?
2. What roles to do you think the sun and the wind might play in a movie? What might they represent? Can you think of where words in the title suggest an underlying theme or presence in some other work of fiction (movie or novel)?

Actividad B   Dos personajes (*characters*)

These are the two main characters you will meet in this episode. Try to determine which of the sentences for each character strikes you as true or likely based on a first impression from the photos.

▲ María Sánchez

1. Es profesora de economía.
2. Es española.
3. Es inteligente y dedicada.

▲ Jaime (James) Talavera

1. Es hombre de negocios (*businessman*).
2. Es español.
3. Es inteligente y sensible (*sensitive*).

Actividad C Un diálogo

In one scene, María speaks to her assistant. Read the dialogue and then select the word that you think best completes it.

MARÍA: ¿Qué quieres,ª Diego?
DIEGO: Sólo quiero decirleᵇ que _____ muy tarde.ᶜ Ya terminamos,ᵈ profesora.

ª¿Qué... *What do you want* ᵇSólo... *I just want to tell you* ᶜ*late* ᵈYa... *We're finished*

a. es   **b.** tienes   **c.** hay

Actividad D El episodio

Now watch the episode. Don't worry if you don't understand everything in Spanish; just try to get the gist of what is going on.

Después de verᵉ el episodio

Actividad A ¿Qué recuerdas? (*What do you remember?*)

Answer each item based on what you remember from watching the **Prólogo.**

1. ¿Cómo se llama el señor que necesita viajar (*needs to travel*) a Chile?
   a. Andy   **b.** John   **c.** James

2. El señor está muy contento (*He is very happy*) con la idea de viajar (*traveling*) a Chile. ¿Cierto (*True*) o falso?
   a. cierto   **b.** falso

3. ¿Cuál es la relación entre María y Diego?
   a. Ella es estudiante y él es profesor.
   b. Él es estudiante y ella es profesora.

4. Probablemente, la especialización (*specialty*) de María es...
   a. matemáticas.   **b.** ingeniería.   **c.** antropología.

Actividad B ¿Lo captaste? (*Did you get it?*)

Go back to **Actividad C** of **Antes de ver el episodio** and verify your answer. Remember: If it helps, watch the corresponding section of the episode again.

Actividad C Utilizando (*Using*) el contexto

One skill you will want to develop as you study Spanish is guessing the meaning of language from context. Here are the first lines of the scene between María and Diego:

DIEGO: Es lindo, ¿no?
MARÍA: Sí. Es muy lindo.

ᵉDespués... *After watching* ᶠDetrás de... *Behind*

Detrás deᶠ la cámara

You probably noticed that one of the main characters is addressed in the **Prólogo** as "James," but his given name (and the name with which he grew up) is "Jaime." Why do you suppose he goes by James, the English equivalent of Jaime? What might this tell you about his character?

Keep this in mind as you watch future episodes of *Sol y viento*. In what other ways may Jaime/James have left his past behind?

Go back and watch this scene again without looking up any words. What are they talking about and what do you think **lindo** means?

Actividad D Intercambio (*Exchange*)

You can use the following adjectives with the verb **ser** to describe some of the characters you have seen in the **Prólogo.** What statements can you make about María, James, Andy, or the **machi?** Share your statements with the class.

1. bilingüe
2. chileno/a (*Chilean*)
3. sabio/a (*wise*)

4. persistente
5. guapo/a (*good-looking*)

▲ María   ▲ Jaime (James)   ▲ Andy   ▲ la machi

Note

You have just completed viewing the **Prólogo** of *Sol y viento* and have worked through the activities in this section. Note that, from here on in, you will view the episodes at least twice. The activities contained in each section are structured in a way to help you do this. Enjoy watching *Sol y viento*!

La llegada^a

Para pensar...

In the first photo, where is Jaime, and who is the man speaking with him? Could he have something to do with the Sol y viento winery?

In the second photo, Jaime is talking on the phone to someone. Where do you think he is? Who is he talking to? And who is the man sitting at the desk in the third photo? What do you think his mood is? Does he look happy? Worried?

 The Interactive CD-ROM to accompany *Sol y viento* contains additional practice with the story of the film and will help you improve your skills in Spanish.

 The *Sol y viento* Online Learning Center Website contains additional practice materials. Log on to **www.mhhe.com/solyviento**.

---

^a*arrival*

SOL Y VIENTO

A primera vista

Antes de ver el episodio

Actividad A ¿Qué recuerdas?

Think briefly about what you know regarding the movie *Sol y viento* thus far. Which of the following are true?

1. ☐ Jaime desea ir (*to go*) a Chile.
2. ☐ Jaime habla inglés y español.
3. ☐ Jaime trabaja para una compañía norteamericana.
4. ☐ María es antropóloga y profesora.
5. ☐ La machi habla de un conflicto.

Actividad B Vocabulario útil (*useful*)

Paso 1 Look over the following words and phrases. You will need them in **Paso 2**.

a propósito	by the way
¡claro que sí!	of course!
para servirlo	at your service
¿qué se le ofrece?	how can I help you?

Paso 2 Using the words and phrases from **Paso 1**, complete the following exchange between a clerk (**empleado**) and a customer (**cliente**).

CLIENTE: Disculpe.[a]
EMPLEADO: _____,[1] señor. _____.[2]
CLIENTE: Busco una camisa de seda.[b] ¿Tienen Uds.?[c]
EMPLEADO: _____.[3] Pase Ud. por aquí, por favor.
CLIENTE: _____:[4] Sólo[d] tengo cheques de viajero.[e] ¿Es problema?
EMPLEADO: No, señor. ¿Tiene Ud. pasaporte?
CLIENTE: Cómo no.[f]

[a]*Excuse me.* [b]*camisa... silk shirt* [c]*¿Tienen... Do you have any?* [d]*Only* [e]*cheques... traveler's checks* [f]*Cómo... Of course.*

Actividad C ¿Qué falta (*is missing*)?

Paso 1 Here is part of the exchange between Mario and Jaime in the hotel lobby that you haven't yet seen or read. Select from the choices below to fill in each blank.

MARIO: _____¹ diez mil pesos, señor.

JAIME: Aquí tiene. _____.² (*Mario turns and walks away. Jaime calls to him.*) ¡Oiga! ¡Espere!

MARIO: ¿Sí, señor? Diga, nomás.^a

JAIME: ¿Ud. hace viajes fuera de^b Santiago?

Detrás de la cámara

As you may recall from the **Prólogo** of *Sol y viento*, Jaime was not too happy about having to go to Chile. He believes that his bilingualism and knowledge of wines were the company's motivating factors for sending him. What is Jaime's background? In a future episode you will hear Jaime talk about himself, but here is some relevant information. He grew up in the Central Valley of California, where his parents and grandparents were farm workers who harvested grapes for the many vineyards in that state. Intelligent and motivated, like many upwardly mobile first-generation children of immigrants, he attended college and graduate school, eventually winding up in the corporate world and leaving his roots and past behind. Or has he?

^aDiga... *Just say the word.* ^b¿Ud.... *Do you take trips outside*

1. **a.** Es
   b. Hay
   c. Son
   d. Están

2. **a.** Por favor (*Please*)
   b. Gracias (*Thank you*)
   c. De nada (*You're welcome*)

Paso 2 Look at the exchange one more time. What do you think Jaime is saying when Mario turns and walks away?

Actividad D   El episodio

Now watch the episode. Remember that it's OK to let some words and expressions slip by you, especially since this is the first time you are watching the episode. You should be able to follow along without understanding every single word. You will watch the episode again in **A segunda vista** (*Upon a second viewing*), and you will understand more then.

Después de ver el episodio

Actividad A   ¿Qué recuerdas?

Answer each item according to what you remember from the episode.

1. Cuando Jaime llega a su habitación (*room*), está cansado (*tired*). ¿Sí o no?
2. ¿Cómo se llama el hotel donde se queda (*is staying*) Jaime?
3. Mañana Jaime necesita ir al Valle del _____.
4. ¿Cuál es el apellido de Jaime? ¿Y el de Mario?
5. En su habitación, Jaime habla por teléfono con...
   a. Andy, de Bartel Aquapower **b.** Carlos Sánchez, de «Sol y viento»
6. ¿Qué palabra describe mejor (*best*) la expresión de Carlos al final?
   a. preocupación (*worry*)   **b.** alegría (*happiness*)
   c. indiferencia

Actividad B   ¿Lo captaste?

Go back to **Actividad C** of **Antes de ver el episodio** to verify your answers. If you need to, watch that particular section of the episode again.

Actividad C   Utilizando el contexto

Paso 1   You have already begun to learn the skill of guessing the meaning of language in context. Did you deduce the meanings of the following phrases in italics? Watch this scene in the episode again if it helps.

> JAIME: Al Hotel Bonaparte. *¿A cuánto sale?*
> MARIO: Eh, um, unos 10.000 (diez mil) pesos, más o menos. *¿Le parece bien?*
> JAIME: Sí. Vamos.

Paso 2   Another skill you have begun to work on is noting that a word or phrase can have multiple meanings. For example, Jaime says **Sí. Vamos.** in response to Mario. **Vamos** means *we go* or *we are going,* but does that make sense in this context? What do you think is the equivalent of **vamos** in this context?

Actividad D   En resumen (*In summary*)

Paso 1   You have now been introduced to Jaime and Mario. How would you describe their personalities, based on your initial impressions? In what ways are they similar, if at all? In what ways are they different? Use adjectives you know to describe each in several sentences.

Paso 2   Share your descriptions with two other people. Decide what you all agree on and present your descriptions to the class. Does everyone else agree?

Nota sobre el lenguaje

One way to express future intent is with the verb **ir** (*to go*) plus the preposition **a** and an infinitive, as in **Voy a ver una película esta noche** (*I'm going to see a movie tonight*). Note, however, that the forms of **ir** are irregular.

voy	vamos
vas	vais
va	van

You will learn more about the uses of **ir** throughout your study of Spanish.

A segunda vista

Antes de ver el episodio

Actividad A ¡A escuchar! (*Let's listen!*)

In a moment you will watch **Episodio 1** once again. But first, familiarize yourself with the following excerpt from the episode in which Jaime calls Carlos at the winery. You will be asked to listen closely and write the missing words in the blanks. Do not look back at any previous excerpts from this episode!

> JAIME: ¿Aló, _____[1] «Sol y viento»?... Don Carlos Sánchez... Ah, _____[2] él. Bien. _____[3] Jaime Talavera, de los Estados Unidos. Compañia Bartel Aquapower... Sí, claro _____[4] hablo español. Ya _____[5] aquí... No, en Santiago. Mañana voy a verlo, _____[6] a mediodía.
>
> CARLOS: _____,[7] señor Talavera. Lo _____[8] mañana. _____[9] entonces. Chau.

Actividad B El episodio

Now watch the episode again. Remember to pay close attention to the scene in which Jaime calls Carlos on the phone and to write down the missing words for **Actividad A.**

Después de ver el episodio

Actividad Intercambio

Offer your opinion on the following questions in English. In later chapters you'll be able to offer such opinions in Spanish.

1. How would you describe Carlos' expression at the end of the episode?
2. Why does he have this expression?

Hint: Keep in mind the boardroom scene from the **Prólogo** when the three men discuss the situation in Chile.

If you need to, watch this scene again and see if you can determine anything by the way Carlos talks as well.

Detrás de la cámara

Mario seems eager to help Jaime at the airport and even boasts by saying that he is **el mejor** (*best*) **chofer de Chile.** If you've taken cabs in this country, you may think he is overly zealous. But Mario is typical of many cab drivers in other countries who hustle to earn a living. Mario works hard to help support a wife and children. He spots Jaime coming out of the airport terminal and realizes, "This could be a good gig." He also knows that business travelers like Jaime often tip well.

SOL Y VIENTO: Enfoque cultural

In **Episodio 1** of *Sol y viento*, Jaime arrives at the airport in Santiago, where he is greeted by an enthusiastic driver, Mario. Santiago, like any major city in the Spanish-speaking world, offers both private drivers like Mario as well as regular public taxis. However, taxi systems and taxi drivers vary from city to city. In Santiago, they are safe, clean, and convenient, and as in any great city there are lots of them. As in this country, in Chile the fare is calculated by meters, and there is no need to negotiate a price (unless you use a private taxi). In Mexico City, in contrast, you generally have to ask how much it will cost to get to your destination before getting in the taxi. If not, you may wind up paying much more than you should, as those taxis may not use meters. Nonetheless, in most Spanish-speaking countries outside of Spain, taxi rides tend to be less expensive than they are in this country.

▲ Hay muchos taxis en México, D.F.*

 # Para escribir

Antes de escribir

For this activity, you will write descriptions of Jaime and Mario, comparing and contrasting them. From the following list of adjectives, decide which ones best describe either character (or both). Share your ideas with someone else.

	ADJETIVOS	JAIME	MARIO
1.	guapo (*handsome*)	☐	☐
2.	ambicioso	☐	☐
3.	simpático (*nice*)	☐	☐
4.	joven (*young*)	☐	☐
5.	inteligente	☐	☐
6.	trabajador (*hard-working*)	☐	☐

*D.F. = **Distrito Federal,** much like Washington, D.C. (District of Columbia)

ADJETIVOS	JAIME	MARIO
7. bilingüe	☐	☐
8. serio	☐	☐
9. gregario	☐	☐
10. reservado	☐	☐

A escribir

Paso 1 Now that you have made some preliminary decisions about the personalities of these two characters, you must decide how you will organize your thoughts. Select one of the following possibilities:

☐ write about Jaime first, then Mario

☐ write about Mario first, then Jaime

☐ use the personality traits to compare and contrast each person as you go

Paso 2 Now draft your description on a separate sheet of paper. The following phrases may be helpful in writing out your descriptions.

al contrario	on the other hand
en cambio	on the other hand
igualmente	equally
no tanto	not as much
pero	but
sin embargo	however
también	also
y	and

Paso 3 Exchange compositions with a classmate so that you can provide initial feedback for each other. As you read each other's composition, check for the following:

☐ overall sense, meaning

☐ adjective/noun agreement

☐ subject/verb agreement

☐ spelling

Al entregar (*Upon handing in*) la composición

Review your classmate's feedback. As you write the final version of your composition, remember to check for the correct use of the following if they appear in your writing, then turn it in to your professor:

☐ descriptive adjectives

☐ present-tense verbs

El encuentro[a]

Para pensar...

In the first photo on this page, Jaime Talavera meets a young woman. Do you think she will have anything to do with Jaime's work in Chile? Or will she have a role in his personal life? Could it have something to do with the piece of paper that Jaime is reading?

In the third photo, we see Mario and Jaime smiling. What do you think they're smiling about? Could it be related to the title of this episode?

 The Interactive CD-ROM to accompany *Sol y viento* contains additional practice with the story of the film and will help you improve your skills in Spanish.

 The *Sol y viento* Online Learning Center Website contains additional practice materials. Log on to **www.mhhe.com/solyviento**.

[a]*encounter*

SOL Y VIENTO

A primera vista

Antes de ver el episodio

Actividad A ¿Qué recuerdas?

Indicate whether the following statements are **cierto** or **falso,** based on what you've seen so far in *Sol y viento.*

	CIERTO	FALSO
1. Jaime tiene ganas de ir a Santiago.	☐	☐
2. Jaime ya sabe (*already knows*) mucho de vinos.	☐	☐
3. Mario no puede llevar a Jaime al Valle del Maipo.	☐	☐
4. El hotel donde Jaime se aloja (*is staying*) se llama Hotel Bonaparte.	☐	☐
5. Jaime necesita hablar con Andrés Sánchez de la viña «Sol y viento».	☐	☐

Actividad B Vocabulario útil

Paso 1 Look over the words and phrases that follow. You will need them in **Paso 2.**

¡espere!	wait!
ojalá que nos veamos de nuevo	I hope we see each other again
¡qué coincidencia!	what a coincidence!

Paso 2 Using the words and phrases from **Paso 1,** complete the following exchange between a man and a woman who have just met.

HOMBRE: Soy Juan Molino y trabajo en la universidad.

MUJER: _____[1] ¡Yo también! Yo trabajo en el departamento de química. ¿En qué departamento trabaja Ud.?

HOMBRE: Soy profesor de biología. ¡Somos vecinos![a] _____[2]

MUJER: Igualmente. Bueno, Juan Molino, tengo que irme.[b]

HOMBRE: _____[3] No sé[c] cómo se llama Ud.

MUJER: ¡Ah, perdón! Soy Alicia Rodríguez.

[a]*neighbors* [b]tengo... *I have to leave* [c]No... *I don't know*

Actividad C   ¿Qué falta?

Here is part of the exchange that you have not yet seen between Jaime, María, and Mario in front of the hotel. Select from the choices to fill in each blank.

MARIO: Buenos días, don Jaime...
¡Lo esperaba!ᵃ

JAIME: Fuiᵇ a _____¹ un poco.
Bueno, hasta aquí llego yo.
¿_____² que la llevemosᶜ a algún sitio?

MARÍA: No, gracias. Mi trabajo _____³ cerca de aquí. Puedo
_____.⁴

ᵃLo... *I was waiting for you!* ᵇ*I went* ᶜque... *us to take you*

1. **a.** charlar   **b.** correr   **c.** levantar pesas (*lift weights*)
2. **a.** Quiere   **b.** Tiene   **c.** Puede
3. **a.** es   **b.** no es   **c.** está
4. **a.** caminar (*walk*)   **b.** hablar   **c.** bailar

Actividad D   El episodio

Now watch the episode. Don't worry if there are things you don't understand. You should be able to follow most of what happens without understanding every single word. You will watch the episode again in **A segunda vista,** and you will understand more then.

Después de ver el episodio

Actividad A   ¿Qué recuerdas?

Answer each question according to what you remember from the episode.

1. ¿Qué ejercicio hace Jaime en el parque?
   a. Juega al fútbol (*soccer*).   **b.** Corre.   **c.** Hace ejercicios aeróbicos.

2. ¿Cuánto cuesta el papelito de la suerte (*fortune*)?

    a. tres pesos   **b.** trece pesos   **c.** trescientos (300) pesos

3. ¿Cómo sabe Jaime el nombre de María? Lo sabe por (*because of*)...

    a. el papelito de la suerte.   **b.** los libros de ella.   **c.** su tarjeta (*card*).

4. María trabaja en dos lugares: en la universidad y en...

    a. el Hotel Bonaparte.   **b.** un sitio de excavación.   **c.** el Parque Forestal.

5. El papelito dice que _____ es un torbellino (*whirlwind*).

    a. el amor   **b.** la antropóloga   **c.** el tiempo

6. Al final del episodio, ¿quién parece (*seems*) tener más interés en el papelito de la suerte?

    a. Jaime   **b.** Mario

Actividad B ¿Lo captaste?

Go back to **Actividad C** of **Antes de ver el episodio** to verify your answers. If you need to, watch that particular section of the episode again.

Actividad C Utilizando el contexto

You have already begun to learn the skill of guessing the meaning of language in context. Did you deduce the meanings of the following phrases in italics? Watch this scene between Jaime, the kid (**el cabrito**), and María again if you think it will help.

JAIME: ¡Le pido mil disculpas! *Andaba distraído.*
CABRITO: El señor *estaba leyendo* el papelito de la suerte.
MARÍA: Ah. Debe ser una suerte excepcional.

Actividad D En resumen

Complete the description of the episode you have just watched by inserting the words and phrases on the right into the appropriate spaces.

En este episodio, Jaime _____[1] en el Parque Forestal. Ve a[a] un hombre que _____[2] papelitos de la suerte. Jaime _____[3] el papelito y de repente[b] _____[4] una mujer. Es María Sánchez. Jaime le pide disculpas[c] y María sigue caminando.[d] Jaime _____[5] caminar con María hasta el Hotel Bonaparte donde Mario lo _____[6] Los tres _____[7] un rato[e] y luego María _____[8] irse.

corre
decide
espera (*waits*)
hablan
lee
necesita
se choca con (*he bumps into*)
vende

[a]Ve... *He sees*   [b]de... *suddenly*   [c]le... *apologizes*   [d]sigue... *keeps walking*
[e]un... *a while*

A segunda vista

Antes de ver el episodio

Actividad A ¡A escuchar!

In a moment you will watch **Episodio 2** once again. Familiarize yourself with the following excerpt from the scene in which Jaime talks with a young boy (**cabrito**) in the park. You will be asked to listen closely and write the missing words in the blank. Do not look back at any previous excerpts from this episode!

JAIME: ¿_____¹ pesos?
CABRITO: ¡Chis! ¡_____² pesos no, señor! ¡Son _____³ pesos!
JAIME: Ah, espere.
CABRITO: _____,⁴ _____⁵ y _____.⁶ Ya, _____.⁷
JAIME: Ah, y _____⁸ cien son para ti.
CABRITO: ¡Gracias, señor!

Actividad B El episodio

Now watch the episode again. Remember to pay close attention to the scene in which Jaime talks to the young boy in the park and to write down the missing words for **Actividad A.**

Después de ver el episodio

Actividad Intercambio

In this episode Jaime reads that love is a whirlwind (**El amor es un torbellino.**). With which of the following statements about love would you agree?

El amor es...

a. un túnel sin salida (*without an exit*).

b. ciego (*blind*).

c. un dolor (*ache, pain*) que no se puede curar.

d. como un accidente. No sabes cuándo va a ocurrir.

Detrás de la cámara

If you watch María carefully, you may have noticed that she has a determined walk. Even when she's in the park, she never strolls leisurely. What might that say about her personality? María is very goal-oriented, and she doesn't stop until she achieves her goals. Jaime seems to pick up on this, and perhaps that is why he is so persistent. Jaime realizes intuitively that María possesses much more than good looks. That's why when Mario says "¡**Bonita la muchacha, don Jaime!**" Jaime emphasizes that she's also intelligent. Do you think Jaime and María would make a good match? Are they too much alike? Too dissimilar? Or is the combination just right?

17

SOL Y VIENTO: Enfoque cultural

City parks abound in Spanish-speaking countries, as they do in this country. However, they are often used in different ways. In **Episodio 2** you watched Jaime as he jogged through the Parque Forestal in Santiago. However, using a public park as a place to exercise is not the norm for most Spanish-speaking people. Instead, parks are often places to socialize, and on Sundays they may flourish with couples and families

of all ages out for an old-fashioned Sunday afternoon stroll (**el paseo**). It is also typical to find vendors of all types in these parks selling everything from cotton candy to balloons, as well as entertainers working for donations, such as the organ-grinding fortune teller with his parrot that you will see in this episode. Some well-known parks in Spanish-speaking cities include the Retiro (Madrid), Lazema (Buenos Aires), and Chapultepec (Mexico City), among others.

▲ El parque Chapultepec (México, D.F.)

Para escribir

Antes de escribir

For this activity, you will describe your first impressions of María and decide if she and Jaime have similar personalities. First, choose the adjectives from the following list that best describe María, according to your first impressions. Then share your ideas with someone else.

Creo que María es...

- ☐ aburrida
- ☐ alegre
- ☐ ambiciosa
- ☐ bonita (*pretty*)
- ☐ desconfiada (*untrusting*)
- ☐ divertida
- ☐ enérgica
- ☐ ingenua (*naive*)
- ☐ inteligente
- ☐ introvertida
- ☐ reservada
- ☐ seria

A escribir

Paso 1 Now that you have made some preliminary decisions about your first impressions of María, decide how you will organize your thoughts. Select one of the following possibilities:

☐ describe each character and then write about how María and Jaime are more similar than different

☐ describe each character and then write about how María and Jaime are more different than similar

Paso 2 Now draft your composition on a separate sheet of paper. The following phrases may be helpful in writing out your descriptions. You should also review the phrases from the **Para escribir** section of **Episodio 1.**

además	furthermore, in addition
creo que...	I think that . . .
me parece que...	it seems to me that . . .
(no) son (muy) parecidos	they're (not) (very) similar

Paso 3 Exchange compositions with a classmate so that you can provide initial feedback for each other. Do you agree with your classmate's assessment of Jaime's and María's personalities? As you read each other's composition, check for the following:

☐ overall sense, meaning

☐ adjective/noun agreement

☐ subject/verb agreement

☐ spelling

Al entregar la composición

Review your classmate's feedback. As you write the final version of your composition, remember to check for the correct use of the following if they appear in your writing, then turn it in to your professor:

☐ verb endings and subject agreement

☐ adjectives

☐ **ser** versus **estar**

A la viña[a]

Para pensar...

Jaime y Mario llegan a la viña «Sol y viento». En una de las fotos, Jaime habla con un hombre. ¿Quién es el hombre? ¿De qué van a hablar?

En otra foto ese hombre ofrece un brindis.[b] ¿Por qué o por quién brinda?

 The Interactive CD-ROM to accompany *Sol y viento* contains additional practice with the story of the film and will help you improve your skills in Spanish.

 The *Sol y viento* Online Learning Center Website contains additional practice materials. Log on to **www.mhhe.com/solyviento**.

[a]A... *To the winery*   [b]ofrece... *offers a toast*

SOL Y VIENTO

A primera vista

Antes de ver el episodio

Actividad A ¿Qué recuerdas?

Indica si las siguientes oraciones son ciertas o falsas según (*according to*) lo que recuerdas del **Episodio 2** de *Sol y viento*.

	CIERTO	FALSO
1. Jaime juega al frisbee en un parque de Santiago.	☐	☐
2. Jaime se choca con María mientras lee un papelito de la suerte.	☐	☐
3. María trabaja en una excavación en el Valle del Maipo.	☐	☐
4. María permite que Jaime se quede con (*keep*) su tarjeta.	☐	☐
5. A Jaime no le importa (*Jaime doesn't care about*) la inteligencia de María.	☐	☐

Actividad B Vocabulario útil

Paso 1 Estudia las siguientes palabras y frases.

la bodega	wine cellar
la botella	bottle
la copa de vino	glass of wine
la cosecha	harvest
el merlot (un vino tinto)	merlot (a red wine)
el tonel	barrel
¡salud!	cheers!
se dejará de producir	it will stop being produced

Paso 2 Empareja (*Match*) cada una de las definiciones con la palabra correspondiente del **Paso 1**.

1. ____ El vino se vende (*is sold*) en este recipiente (*container*).

2. ____ El vino se sirve (*is served*) en esto.

3. ____ Es una habitación (*room*) grande donde se almacenan (*are stored*) los vinos.

4. ____ Es un recipiente de madera (*wood*) donde se añeja (*is aged*) el vino.

5. ____ Son las uvas (*grapes*) después de ser recogidas (*picked*) de las viñas (*vines*).

6. ____ Es un vino tinto.

a. la copa
b. el merlot
c. la cosecha
d. la bodega
e. el tonel
f. la botella

Actividad C ¿Qué falta?

En el **Episodio 3** de *Sol y viento* vas a ver una escena en que Carlos y Jaime toman una copa de vino mientras hablan. A continuación (*Following*) hay unos fragmentos de su diálogo.

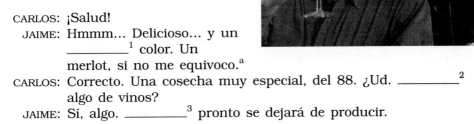

CARLOS: ¡Salud!
  JAIME: Hmmm… Delicioso… y un _____¹ color. Un merlot, si no me equivoco.ª
CARLOS: Correcto. Una cosecha muy especial, del 88. ¿Ud. _____² algo de vinos?
  JAIME: Sí, algo. _____³ pronto se dejará de producir.

ªsi… *if I'm not mistaken*

Indica la respuesta más adecuada para cada espacio en blanco.

1. **a.** tan claro   **b.** excelente   **c.** monótono (*drab*)
2. **a.** dice   **b.** lee   **c.** sabe
3. **a.** Qué bueno que (*Good thing that*)   **c.** Es cierto que (*It's certain that*)
   b. Lástima que (*Too bad that*)

Actividad D El episodio

Ahora mira el episodio. Si hay algo que no entiendes bien, puedes volver a ver la escena en cuestión.

Después de ver el episodio

Actividad A ¿Qué recuerdas?

Contesta cada pregunta basándote en lo que recuerdas del **Episodio 3**.

1. ¿Quién es Traimaqueo?
   a. un miembro de la familia Sánchez   **b.** un trabajador de la viña
2. Don Carlos está nervioso al reunirse con (*upon meeting*) Jaime. ¿Cierto o falso?
   a. cierto   **b.** falso
3. Carlos le dice a Jaime que su madre y su hermana están…
   a. en Santiago.   **b.** en casa.
4. Según Carlos, su hermana no tiene interés en los asuntos (*matters*) de la viña. ¿Cierto o falso?
   a. cierto   **b.** falso
5. Don Carlos y sus trabajadores están planeando…
   a. una recepción para celebrar un vino nuevo.
   b. una fiesta de cumpleaños (*birthday party*).
6. Jaime le dice a don Carlos que la venta (*sale*) tiene que suceder (*happen*) en los próximos días. ¿Cierto o falso?
   a. cierto   **b.** falso

Actividad B ¿Lo captaste?

Vuelve a (*Return to*) la **Actividad C** en **Antes de ver el episodio** para verificar tus respuestas. Si es necesario, vuelve a ver el episodio.

Actividad C Utilizando el contexto

Ya sabes que es difícil interpretar pronombres directos sin contexto. Al ver (*Upon watching*) más episodios de *Sol y viento*, trata de usar tus conocimientos (*knowledge*) del trama (*plot*) para ayudarte a identificar los pronombres. Considera el diálogo a continuación.

JAIME: ¿Le molesta si primero doy[a] un tour por la viña?
CARLOS: No, para nada. Pero yo necesito quedarme aquí en la oficina. Traimaqueo lo puede guiar. Yo lo voy a llamar a su celular. ¿Sabe llegar?

[a]*I take*

Basándote en el contexto, ¿a quién se refiere **lo** en **Traimaqueo lo puede guiar**? ¿Y en **Yo lo voy a llamar a su celular**?

Actividad D En resumen

Completa la narración con las palabras y expresiones apropiadas de la lista.

En este episodio, Jaime visita la viña «Sol y viento», donde _____[1] a don Carlos, el administrador de la viña. Carlos y Jaime _____[2] una copa de vino en la oficina de Carlos mientras[a] _____[3] de finalizar la _____[4] de la viña. Jaime _____[5] finalizarlo todo dentro de[b] pocos días. Sin embargo,[c] Carlos no _____[6] las firmas[d] necesarias, y por eso Jaime _____[7] en no irse del Valle del Maipo sin un _____[8] firmado.[e]

conoce (*he meets*)
contrato
insiste
hablan
quiere
tiene
toman
venta

[a]*while* [b]*dentro... within* [c]*Sin... Nevertheless* [d]*signatures* [e]*signed*

A segunda vista

Antes de ver el episodio

Actividad A ¡A escuchar!

Pronto vas a volver a ver el **Episodio 3.**
Repasa brevemente el siguiente fragmento
del diálogo entre Carlos y Jaime. Cuando
veas el episodio, llena los espacios en
blanco con las palabras correctas. ¡No vuelvas a ver otros fragmentos de este episodio!

> JAIME: Bonita _____.¹
> CARLOS: Y muy buen _____.²
> ¿Quisieraª hacer un breve recorrido?ᵇ ¿Le gusta el _____³?
> JAIME: Sí, me gusta mucho, pero _____⁴ esperar. Tenemos
> negociosᶜ _____.⁵ ¿No es cierto?
> CARLOS: Bueno, sí. Es cierto. ¿Por qué no vamos a mi _____⁶
> para tener así más privacidad?

ªWould you like ᵇtour ᶜbusiness

Actividad B El episodio

Ahora mira el episodio de nuevo. No te olvides de (*Don't forget*) prestar
atención a la escena en que Carlos y Jaime se conocen (*meet each
other*) y apunta (*jot down*) las palabras que faltan para la **Actividad
A.** Puedes mirar el episodio más de una vez si quieres.

Después de ver el episodio

Actividad Intercambio

Paso 1 Con un com-
pañero (una compañera)
de clase, comparen sus
opiniones sobre las si-
guientes preguntas. Si es
necesario, vuelve a ver la
escena en cuestión.

1. ¿Cómo describi-
rían Uds. (*would
you describe*) la
interacción entre
Carlos y Traimaqueo cuando llega Jaime a la viña?

2. ¿Tienen una buena o mala relación? ¿Qué evidencia tienen
para apoyar (*support*) su opinión?

Paso 2 Compartan sus opiniones con la clase. ¿Están todos de
acuerdo con la descripción de la relación entre Carlos y Traimaqueo?

SOL Y VIENTO: Enfoque cultural

En el **Episodio 3,** Jaime y Mario llegan al Valle del Maipo, y Mario compra unas empanadas para Jaime y para él. En muchos países hispanos, sobre todo en Latinoamérica, son típicos estos puestos[a] pequeños donde se vende comida. En Puerto Rico, al lado de algunas carreteras[b] hay puestos con letreros hechos a mano[c] que anuncian «pollo asado y frutas». En México, es típico ver en la ciudad puestos pequeños en forma de «carritos»[d] donde se venden tacos y tortas (sándwiches). En las zonas rurales, son más comunes los lugares pequeños como el puesto en donde Mario compró[e] las empanadas. Este tipo de comida tiene mucha demanda: es barata y se encuentra por todas partes en los países latinos. Pero, lo principal[f] es que les ofrece a personas de pocos recursos[g] la oportunidad de ganar algún dinero.

▲ Unos puestos de comida en México.

[a]*stands* [b]*highways* [c]*letreros... hand-made signs* [d]*carts* [e]*bought* [f]*lo... the main thing* [g]*financial resources*

Para escribir

Antes de escribir

Para esta actividad, vas a escribir una breve composición sobre los gustos (*likes*) de Jaime y de Carlos. Para comenzar, indica si las afirmaciones (*statements*) se refieren a Jaime, a Carlos o a los dos (**ambos**), según lo que crees.

	JAIME	CARLOS	AMBOS
1. Le gusta darse aires (*to put on airs*).	☐	☐	☐
2. Le gusta su trabajo.	☐	☐	☐
3. Le gusta mandar (*to give orders*).	☐	☐	☐
4. No le gusta esperar.	☐	☐	☐
5. Le gusta ir al grano (*to get to the point*).	☐	☐	☐
6. Le gustan los vinos chilenos.	☐	☐	☐
7. Le gustan los negocios.	☐	☐	☐
8. No le gustan las sorpresas (*surprises*).	☐	☐	☐

Nota sobre el lenguaje

You have probably already used **me gusta(n)** to express your likes and dislikes. Although **gustar** is typically translated into English as *to like,* it actually means *to be pleasing to.* To talk about what is pleasing to another person or persons, use **le** or **les** before **gusta(n)**:

A Mario **le gusta** el vino.
Mario likes wine.
(Wine is pleasing to Mario.)

A Mario **le gustan** las empanadas.
Mario likes empanadas.
(Empanadas are pleasing to Mario.)

A María y Diego **les gusta** la antropología.
María and Diego like anthropology.
(Anthropology is pleasing to María and Diego.)

Note that the subject in these sentences comes after **gustar,** not before. In the second sentence, for example, **gustar** agrees with **empanadas,** not **Mario.** You will learn more about **gustar** and other verbs like it throughout your study of Spanish.

A escribir

Paso 1 Ahora que tienes algunas ideas sobre los gustos de cada personaje, ¿cómo vas a organizarlas? Escoge (*Choose*) una de las posibilidades a continuación:

☐ escribir sobre los gustos de Jaime primero, y luego sobre los de (*those of*) Carlos

☐ escribir sobre los gustos de Carlos, y luego sobre los de Jaime

☐ comparar a los dos simultáneamente, según la lista de afirmaciones en el **Paso 1**

Paso 2 Ahora redacta (*draft*) tu composición en una hoja de papel aparte (*separate sheet of paper*). Las siguientes palabras y frases te pueden ser útiles al redactar tu composición.

por otro lado	on the other hand
por un lado	on the one hand
también	also
tampoco	either; neither

Paso 3 Intercambia (*Exchange*) tu composición con la de un compañero (una compañera) de clase. ¿Entiende todo él/ella? ¿Tiene sugerencias para mejorar (*improve*) el contenido o la gramática? Revisa los siguientes puntos:

☐ el significado (*meaning*) y el sentido (*sense*) en general

☐ la concordancia (*agreement*) entre adjetivo y sujeto

☐ la concordancia entre verbo y sujeto

☐ la ortografía (*spelling*)

Al entregar la composición

Usa los comentarios de tu compañero/a de clase para escribir una versión final de tu composición. Repasa (*Review*) los siguientes puntos sobre el lenguaje si aparecen (*they appear*), y luego entrégale la composición a tu profesor(a):

- ☐ el uso correcto de **ser** y **estar**
- ☐ el uso correcto de **le(s) gusta(n)**
- ☐ el uso correcto de los verbos
- ☐ el uso correcto de los adjetivos

Otro encuentro

Para pensar...

Basándote en las fotos, ¿a qué encuentro(s) se refiere el título de este episodio? ¿Quién es el señor que habla con Jaime? ¿De qué están hablando ellos? Y la figura en la mano[a] de Jaime, ¿qué representa? ¿Crees que María está contenta de ver a Jaime de nuevo?

[a]*hand*

 The Interactive CD-ROM to accompany *Sol y viento* contains additional practice with the story of the film and will help you improve your skills in Spanish.

 The *Sol y viento* Online Learning Center Website contains additional practice materials. Log on to **www.mhhe.com/solyviento**.

SOL Y VIENTO

A primera vista

Antes de ver el episodio

Actividad A ¿Qué recuerdas?

¿Qué recuerdas hasta el momento? Escribe el nombre de los personajes apropiados en los espacios. Pero antes de empezar, lee la breve **Nota sobre el lenguaje** que aparece a continuación.

1. Después de correr, _____ compró una fortuna.
2. Al leer (*Upon reading*) su fortuna, se chocó con (*he bumped into*) _____, una profesora de antropología.
3. _____ lo llevó a la viña «Sol y viento». Allí habló con _____ sobre la venta de la viña.
4. No pudo ver a _____. _____ le dijo a Jaime que ella se fue a Santiago.

Nota sobre el lenguaje

If you haven't yet learned the formation of the preterite, one of the past tenses in Spanish, here is a quick guide for talking about someone else's activities in the past:

-ar verbs end in **-ó: habló** (*he/she spoke*), **caminó** (*he/she walked*)

-er/-ir verbs end in **-ió: corrió** (*he/she ran*), **salió** (*he/she went out / left*)

Some frequently used verbs do not follow this pattern, such as **dijo (decir), pudo (poder), estuvo (estar)**, and **fue (ir)**. You will learn more about past tenses throughout your study of Spanish.

Actividad B Vocabulario útil

Paso 1 Estudia las siguientes palabras y frases.

las cepas	vinestocks
los dioses	gods
me enterrarán	they will bury me (I will be buried)
nací	I was born
los pies	feet
púrpura	purple
el regalo	gift
la sangre	blood
se equivocan	(they) fool themselves
el topacio	topaz

Paso 2 Usa las palabras y frases del **Paso 1** para completar cada oración a continuación. **¡OJO!** No se usan todas las palabras y frases.

1. Según algunos, el vino es un _____ de los dioses, algo especial.

2. Para hacer buen vino, son importantes el sol, la tierra y claro, las _____.

3. Soy muy orgulloso (*proud*) de mi lugar de origen. _____ aquí y _____ aquí.

4. Muchas personas _____ porque creen que el dinero hace su vida mejor, pero no siempre es así.

5. El _____ es una piedra (*stone*) preciosa que puede ser de varios colores.

Actividad C ¿Qué falta?

En este episodio, Jaime oye a Traimaqueo decir que doña Isabel lo espera en la casa. Lee el diálogo entre Jaime y Traimaqueo.

YOLANDA: Oye, viejo.* ¿Vas a llegar muy tarde?

TRAIMAQUEO: Un poquito. La señora Isabel me espera en la casa.

JAIME: Creía que la señora Isabel estaba† en Santiago.

TRAIMAQUEO: No, no, no. La señora Isabel no hace muchos viajes en estos días. _____.

¿Qué razón crees que va a ofrecer Traimaqueo para explicar por qué doña Isabel no hace muchos viajes?

a. La señora está muy ocupada (*busy*) con la viña.

b. La señora no está de muy buena salud (*health*).

Actividad D El episodio

Ahora mira el episodio. Si hay algo que no entiendes bien, puedes volver a ver la escena en cuestión.

Después de ver el episodio

Actividad A ¿Qué recuerdas?

Contesta cada pregunta sobre el **Episodio 4.**

1. ¿Quién le dio un tour de la viña a Jaime? ¿Los acompañó Mario?

2. Cuando Jaime oyó que doña Isabel estaba en casa, decidió ir a verla en seguida. ¿Sí o no?

3. ¿Le dijo Carlos la verdad a Jaime? ¿Sí o no?

4. ¿Para quién compró Jaime la figurita del espíritu mapuche?

---

*Viejo/a** is a term of endearment often used among people who have known each other for a long time. It is used more typically among married people.

†**Estaba** is a past-tense verb form, called the *imperfect,* that you will learn about in the next **episodio.** In this context, it means (*she*) *was.*

Actividad B   ¿Lo captaste?

Ahora verifica tu respuesta a la **Actividad C** de **Antes de ver el episodio.** Puedes ver esa escena de nuevo si quieres.

Actividad C   Utilizando el contexto

¿Pudiste deducir el significado de las palabras y expresiones que aparecen *en letra cursiva,* según el contexto en que aparecen?

1.   TRAIMAQUEO: Pasemos a la viña, *¿le parece?*
2.   JAIME: ¿Tiene algún significado esta figurita?
                … *¿A cuánto me sale?*
   TENDERA (*Shopkeeper*): Diecinueve mil quinientos pesos.
       JAIME: Perfecto. *Me la llevo.*

Actividad D   En resumen

Completa la siguiente narración con las palabras y expresiones apropiadas de la lista a la derecha.

En este episodio, Jaime _____¹ la viña «Sol y viento» gracias a un tour que le da Traimaqueo. Al final del tour, Traimaqueo recita parte de un _____² sobre el vino, demostrandoª su _____³ por el vino. Jaime llega a saber que Carlos no es una persona honesta, pues le mintióᵇ sobre su _____.⁴ Más tarde, Jaime tiene un encuentro _____⁵ con María. Ella está en el mercado colocandoᶜ anuncios en apoyoᵈ del _____.⁶ Jaime le da una sorpresa: una figurita del _____⁷ protector de los mapuches. ¿Cómo crees que van las relaciones entre Jaime y María?

agradable
conoce
espíritu (*m.*)
madre
pasión (*f.*)
poema (*m.*)
pueblo mapuche

ªshowing ᵇhe lied ᶜhanging ᵈsupport

A segunda vista

Antes de ver el episodio

Actividad A ¡A escuchar!

Vas a ver el **Episodio 4** de nuevo. Primero, repasa la siguiente escena. Luego, mientras la veas, completa lo que dicen los personajes con las palabras y expresiones que oyes.

> MARÍA: Bueno, además de ser _____,[1] trabajo por los derechos[a] del pueblo mapuche.
> JAIME: ¡Ah! Entonces, a lo mejor le gusta esto. Es _____[2] Ud.
> MARÍA: ¿Para míííí? ¡Oye! ¡Qué _____![3] ¿Cómo sabía... ?
> JAIME: Su _____.[4]
> MARÍA: ¡Ah, por supuesto![b]

[a]*rights* [b]*por... of course*

Actividad B El episodio

Ahora mira el episodio de nuevo. No te olvides de hacer la **Actividad A** en **Antes de ver el episodio** mientras lo ves. Puedes mirar el episodio más de una vez si quieres.

Después de ver el episodio

Actividad Intercambio

Ya sabes que Carlos le mintió a Jaime en cuanto a la ausencia de la señora Isabel. Como clase, comenten las siguientes preguntas.

1. ¿Por qué mintió Carlos? ¿Esconde algo?
2. ¿Hay algún problema en la viña? ¿Cuál es?
3. ¿Qué sabe doña Isabel de la venta de «Sol y viento»?

Detrás de la cámara

Jaime comments on Traimaqueo's evident passion about wine. Traimaqueo does indeed love the land and the winery. He also cares deeply about the family he works for, especially doña Isabel. Traimaqueo and his wife Yolanda have been with the family for a long, long time. Having been with the winery for so long, they both try to keep an eye out for doña Isabel. When doña Isabel's husband died, Traimaqueo felt the need to watch over things in his absence. Yolanda is less conspicuous than Traimaqueo, playing the classic rural female role of servant. She is indeed close to doña Isabel, but she also "knows her place" as a housekeeper. Like Traimaqueo, she is honest and simple. The two of them would do anything for doña Isabel and the winery.

SOL Y VIENTO: Enfoque cultural

En el **Episodio 4,** María coloca carteles[a] para una reunión a favor de los mapuches. Como muchas personas en Latinoamérica, María lucha[b] por los derechos de los grupos indígenas que no tienen voz[c] ni mucha influencia en la política de su país. El activismo por los indígenas no se limita a Chile sino también se observa en México, el Paraguay, Guatemala, el Perú y otros países. Muchas veces estos indígenas no tienen suficiente conocimiento del idioma español, lo cual impide su participación activa en la sociedad. En tales[d] casos necesitan de personas como María que los ayudan a obtener los beneficios que les corresponden según las leyes[e] del país. Además, luchan por un sistema de educación bilingüe o, por lo menos, cursos de español como segunda lengua.

▲ Un indígena ecuatoriano

[a]coloca... *hangs up posters* [b]*fights* [c]*voice* [d]*such* [e]*laws*

Para escribir

Antes de escribir

Paso 1 Para esta actividad, vas a escribir una breve composición sobre los eventos más importantes en *Sol y viento* hasta el momento. Para comenzar, indica (✓) los eventos más importantes para narrar la historia. (Los espacios en blanco son para el **Paso 2.**)

____ ☐ Jaime llegó a Santiago.

____ ☐ Jaime conoció a (*met*) María en el Parque Forestal.

____ ☐ Mario se ofreció (*offered himself*) como chofer.

____ ☐ Jaime llamó a Carlos.

____ ☐ Jaime conoció a Carlos.

____ ☐ Jaime conoció a Yolanda, la esposa de Traimaqueo.

____ ☐ Jaime supo (*found out*) que Carlos le había mentido (*had lied to him*).

____ ☐ Jaime salió a correr.

____ ☐ Carlos le sirvió a Jaime una copa de un vino especial.

____ ☐ Jaime dio con (*ran into*) María otra vez.

____ ☐ Traimaqueo le dio a Jaime una tour de la bodega y de la viña.

____ ☐ Jaime invitó a María a tomar algo y ella aceptó.

Paso 2 Pon (*put*) los eventos que marcaste en orden cronológico. Escribe los números en los espacios en blanco del **Paso 1.**

A escribir

Paso 1 Usa los eventos de **Antes de escribir, Paso 1** para escribir un borrador (*rough draft*) en una hoja de papel aparte. Las palabras y expresiones a continuación pueden serte útiles.

al día siguiente	the next day
después	afterward
después de + (*noun/infinitive*)	after + (*noun/infinitive*)
entonces	then
luego	then
más tarde	later
pero	but
y	and

Paso 2 Mira bien lo que has escrito (*you have written*). ¿Quieres agregar (*to add*) oraciones para hacer la narración más interesante? Por ejemplo, en vez de decir: «Jaime fue al Parque Forestal para correr. Allí conoció a María», escribe algo como «Jaime fue a correr en el Parque Forestal donde conoció a María, una mujer joven, atractiva e inteligente».

Paso 3 Intercambia tu composición con la de un compañero (una compañera) de clase para saber sus comentarios. Revisa los siguientes puntos:

- ☐ el significado y el sentido en general
- ☐ la concordancia entre sustantivo y adjetivo
- ☐ la concordancia entre sujeto y verbo
- ☐ la ortografía

Al entregar la composición

Usa los comentarios de tu compañero/a de clase para escribir una versión final de tu composición. Repasa los siguientes puntos sobre el lenguaje y luego entrégasela a tu profesor(a):

- ☐ la forma correcta de los verbos en el pretérito
- ☐ el uso correcto de pronombres de complemento directo e indirecto para evitar la repetición
- ☐ el uso correcto de palabras de transición (**luego, después, pero,** etcétera)

Un día perfecto

Para pensar...

Basándote en las fotos, ¿por qué crees que este episodio se llama «Un día perfecto»? ¿Para quién o para quiénes es «perfecto» el día? ¿Quién es la mujer que habla con Carlos? ¿Dónde están? ¿De qué estarán hablando?[a]

[a]estarán... *must they be talking about*

 The Interactive CD-ROM to accompany *Sol y viento* contains additional practice with the story of the film and will help you improve your skills in Spanish.

 The *Sol y viento* Online Learning Center Website contains additional practice materials. Log on to **www.mhhe.com/solyviento**.

SOL Y VIENTO

A primera vista

Antes de ver el episodio

Actividad A ¿Qué recuerdas?

¿Recuerdas lo que viste en el **Episodio 4**? Indica si las oraciones a continuación son ciertas o falsas. Si la oración es falsa, cámbiala.

		CIERTO	FALSO
1.	Jaime pudo conocer a doña Isabel.	☐	☐
2.	Carlos le regaló a Jaime una botella de vino.	☐	☐
3.	Diego no sabe si va a continuar con sus estudios por presiones familiares.	☐	☐
4.	La figura que compró Jaime simboliza un espíritu azteca.	☐	☐
5.	Jaime y María quedaron en reunirse en el bar del hotel de Jaime.	☐	☐

Actividad B Vocabulario útil

Paso 1 Estudia las siguientes palabras y frases.

la Bolsa (de valores)	stock market
el brindis / brindemos	toast (*when drinking*) / let's toast
los campesinos	farm workers
las exportaciones	exports
los remolinos	pinwheels
te encargaste de	you took over, assumed responsibility for
Ud. no se limita a	you don't limit yourself to
vamos a tutearnos	let's use the **tú** form with each other

Paso 2 Usa las palabras y frases del **Paso 1** para completar cada oración a continuación. **¡OJO!** No se usan todas las palabras y frases.

1. _____ trabajan la tierra.
2. _____ puede cambiar rápidamente.
3. ¿_____ los asuntos financieros de la compañía?
4. _____ por la salud y por los amigos.
5. _____ porque no me gusta ser tan formal.

Nota sobre el lenguaje

If you haven't yet learned the formation of the imperfect, another past tense in Spanish, here is a quick guide for talking about what someone *was doing* or what *was going on* before another event occurred in the past:

> **-ar** verbs end in **-aba: hablaba** (*he/she was speaking*), **caminaba** (*he/she was walking*)
>
> **-er/-ir** verbs end in **-ía: corría** (*he/she was running*), **salía** (*he/she was leaving*)

There are only three irregular verbs in the imperfect: **ir, ser,** and **ver.** To talk about what someone was doing or what was going on using these verbs, the forms are **iba (ir), era (ser),** and **veía (ver).** You will learn more about the imperfect throughout your study of Spanish.

Actividad C ¿Qué falta?

A continuación hay parte de una conversación entre doña Isabel y Carlos que no has visto (*that you haven't seen*). Antes de ver el episodio, escoge la opción apropiada para llenar cada espacio en blanco.

CARLOS: Mamá, ¿qué te parecería si vendiéramos[a] la viña?

ISABEL: ¿Vender «Sol y viento»? ¿Tú sabes cuánto _____[1] tu papá, cuánto _____[2] yo, para tener esta viña? ¡_____[3] este país sin nada!

[a]¿qué... *how would you feel if we sold*

1. **a.** trabajaba   **b.** trabajó   **c.** trabaja
2. **a.** trabajaba   **b.** trabajé   **c.** trabajo
3. **a.** Vinimos a   **b.** Vivimos en   **c.** Salimos de

Actividad D El episodio

Ahora mira el episodio. Si hay algo que no entiendes bien, puedes volver a ver la escena en cuestión.

Después de ver el episodio

Actividad A ¿Qué recuerdas?

Contesta cada pregunta según lo que recuerdas del episodio.

1. ¿Qué hacía Jaime mientras esperaba a María?
    a. Hablaba por teléfono con Andy.
    b. Leía un artículo en el periódico.
2. Jaime piensa que María tiene una vida más interesante que la suya.
    a. cierto   **b.** falso
3. ¿Con quién habló Isabel después de la salida (*exit*) de Carlos?

4. ¿Qué significa la palabra **mapuche**?

5. ¿En qué trabajaba Jaime en su juventud?

   a. Trabajaba en la exportación de los vinos.

   b. Trabajaba en la fermentación de los vinos.

6. María tiene muchos amigos norteamericanos.

   a. cierto   **b.** falso

7. ¿Por qué colgó (*hung up*) el teléfono Jaime mientras hablaba con Andy?

   a. Porque había una mala conexión.

   b. Porque no quería seguir hablando con Andy.

Actividad B   ¿Lo captaste?

Ahora verifica tus respuestas a la **Actividad C** en **Antes de ver el episodio.** Puedes ver esa escena de nuevo si quieres.

Actividad C   En resumen

Completa la siguiente narración con las palabras y expresiones apropiadas de la lista a la derecha.

En este episodio, las cosas _____^{1} con la viña. Carlos le dice a su madre que _____^{2} «Sol y viento», pero a doña Isabel _____^{3} la idea.

    Mientras tanto,^{a} Jaime y María _____^{4} la tarde juntos. Hablan de sus profesiones y a Jaime _____^{5} el trabajo de María es más interesante que el suyo. Mientras toman una copa de vino, Jaime _____^{6} a María por qué sabe tanto de los vinos. Las cosas _____^{7} entre ellos hasta que María recibe una llamada de Diego y tiene que salir. Pero antes de despedirse^b _____^{8} un beso^c a Jaime.

le cuenta
le da
le parece que
no le gusta nada
no van bien
pasan
quiere vender
van bien

^{a}Mientras... *In the meantime* ^{b}*saying good-bye* ^{c}*kiss*

A segunda vista

Antes de ver el episodio

Actividad A   ¡A escuchar!

En un momento, vas a ver el **Episodio 5** de nuevo. Repasa la siguiente escena. Luego, mientras la ves, completa lo que dicen los personajes con las palabras que faltan.

> ISABEL: ¡Hijo! Me _____ [1] dormida. ¿Te _____ [2] algo, hijo?
>
> CARLOS: No, nada. ¿Por qué?
>
> ISABEL: Sí, algo te _____ [3] Soy tu mamá y te _____ [4] mejor que nadie.
>
> CARLOS: Entonces sabrás[a] que _____ [5] mucho trabajo con la viña, mamá.
>
> ISABEL: Cuando _____ [6] tu papá, te _____ [7] de los negocios. Yo ya _____ [8] vieja y tu hermana _____ [9] otros intereses.

[a]*you should know*

Actividad B   El episodio

Ahora mira el episodio. No te olvides de hacer la **Actividad A** mientras lo ves. Puedes mirar el episodio más de una vez si quieres.

Después de ver el episodio

Actividad   Intercambio

Paso 1   En este episodio conociste a doña Isabel, la madre de Carlos. Piensa en lo siguiente y contesta las preguntas según tu propia opinión.

1. Doña Isabel le dijo a su hijo que había venido (*she had come*) a Chile sin nada. ¿De dónde vino, originalmente?
2. ¿Por qué no quiere vender la viña doña Isabel?
3. ¿Crees que doña Isabel debe hacer lo que quiere su hijo? ¿Por qué sí o por qué no?

Paso 2   Basándote en las respuestas del **Paso 1**, ¿qué adjetivos usarías (*would you use*) para describir a doña Isabel?

Detrás de la cámara

Did you notice who kissed whom first in this episode? As you have seen in previous episodes, Jaime is someone who likes to be in control of situations; however, his budding relationship with María is different. She seems to be the one in control. Although Jaime is not used to a woman taking the initiative in relationships, he doesn't complain!

SOL Y VIENTO: Enfoque cultural

En el **Episodio 5** viste un parque con una estatua enorme de la Virgen María. Los habitantes de Chile son, en su mayoría, católicos, como en la mayoría de los demás países hispanos. Por ejemplo, en España el 94% de la población es católica; en Chile, el 89%; en Venezuela, el 96%; y en Puerto Rico, el 85%.* Hasta en la Guinea Ecuatorial, donde hay una fuerte influencia de las culturas africanas, la mayoría de las personas se identifica con la Iglesia católica. Compara esas cifras[a] con el número de personas estadounidenses que se identifican como católicos: sólo llega al 28%. Claro, la manera en que se practica el catolicismo varía de país a país. Por ejemplo, en México la devoción a la Virgen de Guadalupe es casi más fuerte que la devoción a Jesucristo. Y en la zona andina (el Perú, Bolivia, el Ecuador) los indígenas han forjado[b] un catolicismo con restos[c] de la mitología y creencias de sus antepasados,[d] los inca.

[a]*numbers* [b]*han... have created* [c]*remnants* [d]*ancestors*

▲ La estatua de la Virgen María en el Cerro San Cristóbal en Santiago.

Para escribir

Antes de escribir

Paso 1 Para esta actividad, vas a escribir una breve composición sobre los eventos del día perfecto desde el punto de vista (*point of view*) de María o de Jaime. Para comenzar, indica quién de los dos diría (*would say*) las siguientes oraciones. **¡OJO!** En algunos casos puede ser los dos. (Los espacios en blanco son para el **Paso 2**.)

		JAIME	MARÍA
1.	___ La esperaba (*I was waiting*) en la entrada (*entrance*) del funicular.	☐	☐
2.	___ Leía un artículo con mi foto cuando llegué.	☐	☐
3.	___ ¡Me besó (*kissed*)!	☐	☐
4.	___ Se me olvidó (*I forgot*) por completo mi cita con Diego.	☐	☐
5.	___ Pensé que tenía otro novio (*boyfriend*).	☐	☐
6.	___ Tomamos una copa de vino y hablamos un poco de mi familia.	☐	☐
7.	___ Lo pasábamos muy bien cuando llamó Diego.	☐	☐
8.	___ Tuvo que salir.	☐	☐

*C.I.A. World Fact Book, 2003.

		JAIME	MARÍA

9. ____ Fue un día perfecto.   ☐   ☐

10. ____ Su trabajo me parecía muy interesante.   ☐   ☐

11. ____ Mientras subíamos en el funicular   ☐   ☐
hablábamos de su trabajo y del mío.

Paso 2 Ahora decide si vas a narrar los eventos del día desde la perspectiva de Jaime o de María. Primero, pon los eventos del **Paso 1** en orden cronológico. Escribe los números en los espacios en blanco del **Paso 1.**

A escribir

Paso 1 Usa los eventos del **Paso 1** de **Antes de escribir** para escribir un borrador en una hoja de papel aparte. Puedes utilizar las oraciones del personaje que *no* elegiste para dar más información, pero recuerda que vas a tener que cambiar algunos pronombres y verbos. Las palabras y expresiones a continuación pueden serte útiles.

de repente	suddenly
desafortunadamente	unfortunately
después	afterward
después de + (*noun/infinitive*)	after + (*noun/infinitive*)
entonces	then
luego	then
más tarde	later
pero	but
por fin	finally
y	and

Paso 2 Mira bien lo que has escrito. ¿Quieres agregar palabras, expresiones u oraciones para hacer la narración más interesante?

Paso 3 Intercambia tu composición con la de un compañero (una compañera) de clase para saber sus comentarios. Revisa los siguientes puntos:

- ☐ el significado y el sentido en general
- ☐ la concordancia entre sustantivo y adjetivo
- ☐ la concordancia entre sujeto y verbo
- ☐ la ortografía

Al entregar la composición

Usa los comentarios de tu compañero/a de clase para escribir una versión final de tu composición. Repasa los siguientes puntos sobre el lenguaje y luego entrégasela a tu profesor(a):

- ☐ la narración en el pasado (imperfecto y pretérito)
- ☐ el uso correcto de los pronombres de complemento directo e indirecto
- ☐ el uso correcto de palabras de transición

Confrontación

Para pensar...

En una de las fotos, María está por abrazar a[a] un hombre. ¿Quién es ese hombre con María? ¿Cuál es su relación con ella?

En otra foto, Jaime está hablando con doña Isabel Sánchez. ¿Crees que a ella le cae bien[b] la idea de vender la viña?

En otra foto, María se enoja[c] con Jaime. ¿Por qué crees que está enojada María? ¿Qué ha hecho[d] Jaime?

[a]está... *is about to hug* [b]a... *she likes* [c]se... *gets angry* [d]ha... *has done*

 The Interactive CD-ROM to accompany *Sol y viento* contains additional practice with the story of the film and will help you improve your skills in Spanish.

 The *Sol y viento* Online Learning Center Website contains additional practice materials. Log on to **www.mhhe.com/solyviento**.

SOL Y VIENTO

A primera vista

Antes de ver el episodio

Actividad A ¿Qué recuerdas?

Indica si las siguientes oraciones sobre la trama (*plot*) de *Sol y viento* son ciertas o falsas.

	C	F
1. María trabaja por los derechos de la comunidad mapuche.	☐	☐
2. Los padres de Jaime también eran personas de negocios.	☐	☐
3. Doña Isabel está de acuerdo con Carlos en vender la viña porque es demasiado (*too much*) trabajo mantenerla (*to maintain it*).	☐	☐
4. Carlos cree que la familia lo obligó a encargarse de (*take over*) la viña.	☐	☐
5. María y Jaime lo pasaron muy bien en la cita.	☐	☐

Detrás de la cámara

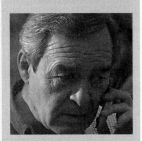

In **Episodio 6** of *Sol y viento* you will meet don Francisco (Paco) Aguilar, an old friend of the Sánchez family and owner of a fine restaurant in Mexico City. In addition to being a restaurateur, don Paco is also a distributor of fine wines. His job is to make contacts with wineries throughout the world and import their products into Mexico. He established a relationship with the Sánchez family many years ago on a trip through the Maipo Valley. He was so impressed with the wine produced at Sol y viento that he made it the house wine at his establishment.

Nota sobre el lenguaje

By now you have seen many command forms, both formal and informal as well as affirmative and negative. If you haven't yet learned the formation of commands, here is a quick guide, using the verb **hablar**. Note how in some instances the "opposite" vowel is used at the end of the verb (a → e, e/i → a).

	AFFIRMATIVE	NEGATIVE
tú	Habl**a** más fuerte.	No habl**es** tan fuerte.
vosotros/as	Habl**ad** más fuerte.	No habl**éis** tan fuerte.
Ud.	Habl**e** más fuerte.	No habl**e** tan fuerte.
Uds.	Habl**en** más fuerte.	No habl**en** tan fuerte.

In the preceding examples, the affirmative commands all mean *Speak louder*, whereas the negative commands mean *Don't speak so loudly*.

There are also many irregular forms for both formal and informal affirmative and negative commands, which you will learn throughout your study of Spanish.

Actividad B Vocabulario útil

Paso 1 Estudia las siguientes palabras y frases.

¡así me gustan!	that's how I like them!
déme...	give me . . .
el jitomate	a type of red tomato (*Mex.*)
el mercado	market
¡pruébelos!	try them!
¿qué tal están... ?	how are . . . ?
¡Ud. debería de saber!	You should know!

Paso 2 Usa las palabras y frases del **Paso 1** para completar el diálogo entre un mesero (*waiter*) y un cliente **¡OJO!** No se usan todas las palabras y frases.

MESERO: ¡Bienvenido,[a] don Pedro! ¿Le gustaría[b] pedir algo?

CLIENTE: ¡Claro que sí! El menú dice que hoy tienen _____[1] rellenos[c] como especialidad de la casa.

MESERO: Es cierto. ¿Los quiere pedir?

CLIENTE: Hmm... _____[2]

MESERO: Están bien deliciosos. El chef los prepara con una salsa picante[d] pero sabrosa.[e] _____[3]

CLIENTE: Está bien. Me ha convencido.[f] _____[4] la especialidad de la casa, por favor.

[a]*Welcome* [b]*¿Le... Would you like* [c]*stuffed* [d]*spicy* [e]*tasty* [f]*Me... You've convinced me.*

Actividad C ¿Qué falta?

A continuación hay un fragmento de una conversación telefónica que tiene don Paco.

PACO: ¿Bueno?[a]... ¿Bueno?... ¡Si no lo oigo bien! ¡_____[1] más fuerte!... ¿Bueno?... ¿Bueno?... Sí, _____[2] tantito[b]... ¿Bueno?... ¿Con quién?... ¡Ah, Isabel! ¡Qué sorpresa!

[a]*Hello? (Mex.)* [b]*a second (coll.)*

Escoge entre las palabras que siguen la más apropiada para cada espacio en blanco.

1. **a.** Hable
   b. Habla
2. **a.** espérame
   b. espéreme

Actividad D El episodio

Ahora mira el episodio. Si hay algo que no entiendes bien, puedes volver a ver la escena en cuestión.

Después de ver el episodio

Actividad A ¿Qué recuerdas?

Contesta cada pregunta a continuación según lo que recuerdas del episodio.

1. ¿A quién llama por teléfono doña Isabel?
   a. a Jaime, en su hotel   **b.** a don Paco, en México
2. ¿Cuál es la relación entre don Paco y María?
   a. Son amigos.   **b.** Son parientes.
3. Jaime se da cuenta de que María y Carlos son _____.
   a. primos   **b.** hermanos   **c.** cuñados
4. Jaime está harto de (*fed up with*) los pretextos (*excuses*) de Carlos y demanda _____ de la familia.
   a. las bodegas   **b.** las firmas   **c.** las cosechas
5. María comprende que Jaime no sabía quién era Carlos y lo perdona.
   a. cierto   **b.** falso

Actividad B ¿Lo captaste?

Vuelve a la **Actividad C** de **Antes de ver el episodio** para verificar tus respuestas. Si es necesario, vuelve a ver la escena en cuestión.

Actividad C Utilizando el contexto

Paso 1 Ya sabes que la frase **¿Qué tal?** es un saludo que quiere decir algo como *How's it going?* Repasa lo que dice don Paco en el mercado a continuación. ¿Qué crees que significa **¿Qué tal... ?** en este contexto?

> PACO: ¡Buenas, doña Lourdes! ¿*Qué tal* están sus jitomates hoy?

Paso 2 A diferencia de otros hispanos, los mexicanos dicen **¿Bueno?** al contestar el teléfono. ¿Qué dice Jaime cuando contesta su teléfono celular? ¿Sabes lo que dicen los españoles? Si no, pregúntaselo a tu profesor(a).

Actividad D En resumen

Llena los espacios en blanco con las palabras a la derecha para completar el resumen del episodio que acabas de ver (*you just saw*).

En este episodio, doña Isabel _____[1] por lo que pasa en la viña. Por eso le pide ayuda a don Francisco (Paco) Aguilar, un amigo de la familia que vive en México. Se nota que a María _____[2] su «tío» Paco y que _____[3] mucho. Entretanto,[a] Jaime va a la viña donde _____[4] doña Isabel, la madre de Carlos. Doña Isabel afirma que «Sol y viento» no _____[5] y Jaime y Carlos entran en una conversación agitada. Luego, María llega del _____[6] con don Paco y presencia[b] la confrontación. Pensando que Jaime la está engañando,[c] María se enoja[d] y deja caer[e] _____[7] que Jaime le regaló.

aeropuerto
el amuleto
conoce a
está a la venta
está preocupada (*worried*)
le cae bien
lo respeta

[a]*Meanwhile* [b]*she witnesses* [c]*deceiving* [d]*se... gets angry* [e]*deja... drops*

A segunda vista

Antes de ver el episodio

Actividad A   ¡A escuchar!

Repasa brevemente el siguiente fragmento de un diálogo entre Jaime y Carlos. Llena los espacios en blanco con las palabras correctas mientras ves el episodio.

> JAIME: ¡Esta cosa no va a funcionar! _____[1] prometió[a] las firmas de su madre, de su hermana y de los vecinos. ¡A que _____[2] ha hecho nada con la comunidad mapuche! Así es, ¿no? ¡La verdad es que no tiene nada! ¡Mi compañía quiere estas _____[3]!
>
> CARLOS: Por favor, _____[4] un par de días más. Se las voy a conseguir.
>
> JAIME: Tenemos que firmar el contrato esta semana... ¡y Ud. no tiene la influencia _____[5]!
>
> CARLOS: Ya _____:[6] yo voy a convencer a mi madre ¡y a mi _____[7] le da lo mismo![b]
>
> JAIME: ¡Lo dudo![c] Según lo que _____[8] y he oído, ¡pienso que a su hermana sí le _____[9] el destino de estas tierras!

[a]*you promised*   [b]*le... doesn't care*   [c]*I doubt*

Actividad B   El episodio

Ahora vas a ver el episodio de nuevo. Presta atención especial a la escena en que Carlos y Jaime discuten (*argue*) y apunta las palabras que faltan para la **Actividad A.** Puedes mirar el episodio más de una vez si quieres.

Después de ver el episodio

Actividad   Intercambio

Ya sabes que Jaime y María tuvieron una confrontación horrible. Entre todos, comenten las siguientes preguntas.

1. ¿Qué creen Uds. que piensa María de la relación entre su hermano y Jaime? ¿De quién sospecha (*is she suspicious*) más, de Carlos o de Jaime?

2. ¿Cuál creen que es la causa principal de su enojo (*anger*), la venta de las tierras familiares? ¿las consecuencias de la venta para los mapuches? ¿la decepción que siente con respecto a Jaime?

3. ¿Cómo puede resolverse esta situación difícil? Apunten algunas ideas.

Detrás de la cámara

Another reason Jaime is so successful at what he does is that he doesn't wait for things to happen—he makes them happen. Jaime quickly gets the hint that Carlos has no real game plan for getting his mother and sister to sign the contract. When he finds out from Traimaqueo that Carlos's mother, doña Isabel, was in the house all along and not in Santiago as Carlos had told him, he circumvents Carlos altogether and goes straight to doña Isabel. Suspecting something is awry, doña Isabel agrees to speak to him.

SOL Y VIENTO: Enfoque cultural

Has visto que en el **Episodio 6,** Jaime le dice a Carlos: «¡A que tampoco ha hecho nada con la comunidad mapuche!» Evidentemente, Carlos había prometido[a] conseguir las tierras de los mapuches que vivían en la zona. En cambio,[b] su hermana María lucha[c] por esa comunidad indígena para preservar su cultura.

El indigenismo y los derechos de los indígenas en Latinoamérica son temas muy importantes en muchos países como el Perú, Chile, México y otros. Por seis siglos los indígenas han sufrido discriminación que los ha mantenido en las capas[d] más bajas de la sociedad. Afortunadamente, en el siglo XX empezó a demostrarse interés[e] en el indigenismo a través del arte del mexicano Diego Rivera y el novelista ecuatoriano Jorge Icaza, entre otros. En el Perú empezaron a reconocer la importancia de ofrecer a los indígenas educación en su lengua nativa, el quechua, y establecieron programas de educación bilingüe en el año 1972. Es más,[f] en 1979 la constitución peruana reconoció el español como lengua oficial del país, pero a la vez que el quechua forma parte integral de la cultura del país, y los dos idiomas quedaron como lenguas oficiales, con restricciones. Aun con estos avances, la situación no está completamente resuelta.[g] Por ejemplo, en 1994 los indígenas del estado mexicano de Chiapas se sublevaron[h] contra el gobierno, reclamando más tierra y más inclusión en el sistema político. Seguramente, la situación de los grupos minoritarios indígenas seguirá siendo[i] un tema central en varios países hispanos por muchos años.

▲ El indigenismo sigue siendo un tema central en la vida de los indígenas, como estas en el Ecuador.

[a]promised [b]En... *On the other hand*
[c]fights [d]layers [e]empezó... *interest began to appear* [f]Es... *What's more* [g]resolved
[h]se... *rose up* [i]seguirá... *will continue to be*

Para escribir

Antes de escribir

Para esta actividad, vas a escribir una composición sobre los eventos más importantes que han ocurrido entre Jaime y María hasta el momento. Describe cómo se sentían (*felt*) Jaime y María en cada situación a continuación.

MODELO: Jaime conoció a María. →
Jaime estaba cansado de correr, pero estaba muy contento. María se sentía... porque...

1. Jaime se chocó con María en el parque.

   _____

2. Jaime vio a María cuando fue de compras en el mercado.

   _____

3. María y Jaime tomaron vino en el café al aire libre (*outdoor*).

   _____

4. María tiró al suelo (*threw down*) el amuleto que Jaime le regaló.

   _____

A escribir

Paso 1 Usa la información de **Antes de ver el episodio** para escribir un borrador en una hoja de papel aparte. Las palabras y expresiones a continuación pueden serte útiles.

a la vez	at the same time
además (de)	in addition (to)
después	afterward
entonces	then
luego	then
más tarde	later
mientras	while
por lo tanto	therefore

Paso 2 Mira bien lo que has escrito. ¿Quieres agregar palabras, expresiones u oraciones para hacer la narración más interesante?

Paso 3 Intercambia tu composición con la de un compañero (una compañera) de clase para saber sus comentarios. Revisa los siguientes puntos:

☐ el significado y el sentido en general
☐ la concordancia entre sustantivo y adjetivo
☐ la concordancia entre sujeto y verbo
☐ la ortografía

Al entregar la composición

Usa los comentarios de tu compañero/a de clase para escribir una versión final de tu composición. Repasa los siguientes puntos sobre el lenguaje y luego entrégasela a tu profesor(a):

☐ el uso correcto del pretérito y del imperfecto
☐ el uso correcto de palabras de transición

Bajo el sol

Para pensar...

En una de las fotos Jaime y Mario sufren un pequeño accidente. ¿Adónde iban? ¿Qué les pasó?

En otras fotos Jaime está con doña Isabel y don Paco. ¿Crees que les ha convencido Jaime[a] a vender la viña? ¿Qué crees que pasa en la escena? ¿Están todos contentos?

[a]les... *Jaime has convinced them*

The Interactive CD-ROM to accompany *Sol y viento* contains additional practice with the story of the film and will help you improve your skills in Spanish.

The *Sol y viento* Online Learning Center Website contains additional practice materials. Log on to **www.mhhe.com/solyviento**.

SOL Y VIENTO

A primera vista

Antes de ver el episodio

Actividad A ¿Qué recuerdas?

Indica si las siguientes oraciones son ciertas o falsas, según lo que sabes de la trama (*plot*) de *Sol y viento*.

		CIERTO	FALSO
1.	Don Paco es dueño de un restaurante en Chile.	☐	☐
2.	El esposo de doña Isabel ya ha muerto.	☐	☐
3.	Doña Isabel llama a don Paco porque se preocupa por la viña.	☐	☐
4.	Ahora Jaime sabe que Carlos y María son hermanos.	☐	☐
5.	María sigue respetando a Jaime aunque sabe que trabaja para Bartel Aquapower.	☐	☐

Actividad B Vocabulario útil

Paso 1 Estudia las siguientes palabras y frases.

arregla	(he) fixes
atraviesa por	(one) travels through
los hechos	deeds
pinchó / ponchó*	(it) punctured
la represa	dam
el repuesto	spare tire
la rueda	tire

Paso 2 Usa las palabras del **Paso 1** para completar cada oración a continuación. **¡OJO!** No se usan todas las palabras y frases.

1. Hoover es el nombre de una _____ grande en los Estados Unidos.
2. Michelin y Goodyear son marcas (*brand names*) populares de _____.
3. Para ir en coche de Los Ángeles, California, a Las Vegas, Nevada, uno _____ el desierto Mojave.
4. La rueda que se saca del baúl (*trunk*) de un auto en casos de emergencia es _____.
5. Generalmente _____ de una persona influyen mucho en nuestra opinión de esa persona.

---

*The use of **pinchar** (by Mario) and **ponchar** (by Jaime) is just one example of many dialectical differences that exist in the Spanish-speaking world.

Actividad C ¿Qué falta?

En el **Episodio 7** Jaime y Mario van a hablar del tiempo que falta para llegar a «Sol y viento». Llena los espacios en blanco con las opciones a continuación. Puedes verificar tus respuestas después de ver el episodio.

JAIME: ¿Estamos lejos?
MARIO: En automóvil, a siete minutos. A pie, cuarenta y cinco minutos, más o menos. Menos si se toma _____[1] por ahí...
JAIME: Me voy a pie. Nos vemos en la viña.
MARIO: ¡Don Jaime! ¡El sol está picando fuerte![a] ¡Que no le dé _____[2]!

1. **a.** la autopista (*highway*)
   b. un atajo (*shortcut*)
2. **a.** un infarto (*heart attack*)
   b. una insolación (*heatstroke*)

[a]picando... *really beating down*

Actividad D El episodio

Ahora mira el episodio. Si hay alguna escena que no entiendes bien, vuelve a verla.

Después de ver el episodio

Actividad A ¿Qué recuerdas?

Contesta las preguntas a continuación según lo que recuerdas del **Episodio 7.**

1. Mario no pudo arreglar la rueda pinchada porque no tenía...
   a. herramientas (*tools*) **b.** gato (*tire jack*) **c.** repuesto

2. Jaime sufrió una insolación antes de llegar a la casa de los Sánchez. ¿Cierto o falso?
   a. cierto **b.** falso

3. Según don Paco, Bartel Aquapower hizo mucho daño a la ecología de este país.
   a. el Brasil **b.** Bulgaria **c.** Bolivia

4. Jaime renuncia a (*quits*) su trabajo con Bartel Aquapower. ¿Cierto o falso?
   a. cierto **b.** falso

5. Doña Isabel le dijo a Jaime que María no _____ fácilmente.
   a. se enamora **b.** perdona **c.** se divierte

Actividad B ¿Lo captaste?

Vuelve a la **Actividad C** de **Antes de ver el episodio** para verificar tus respuestas. Si es necesario, vuelve a ver la escena en cuestión.

Have you noticed that
while María and Jaime
switched to the use of **tú**
in a previous episode,
Mario has continued to
use **usted** with Jaime?
Even though Mario feels
the need to comment on
María and Jaime's rela-
tionship, he and Jaime are
not friends and are not of
the same age group.
Mario is, in effect, an employee of Jaime's. How-
ever, Jaime does use **tú**
when addressing Mario.
You may also have noticed
that Traimaqueo uses **tú**
with Carlos, although he is
technically employed by
the family. What is different here is that
Traimaqueo has known
Carlos since the latter was
a little boy. The use of **tú**
was natural in that adult–
child relationship. That
Traimaqueo now works for
Carlos has not changed
that fundamental and ear-
lier pattern of interaction.
María, of course, when
finding out what Jaime
has been up to, immedi-
ately drops the **tú** and re-
verts to **usted**. Did you
catch this in the previous
episode?

Actividad C En resumen

Llena los espacios en blanco con las palabras a la derecha para completar el resumen del **Episodio 7.**

En este episodio, a Mario y Jaime _____¹ una rueda camino a la viña. Como Mario no tenía _____,² Jaime decidió seguir a pie. En ruta a la viña, Jaime sufrió una _____³ y se desmayó.ᵃ Mientras Jaime se recuperaba en casa de doña Isabel, don Paco _____⁴ que Bartel Aquapower quería construir una represa en el valle, lo cual le haríaᵇ mucho daño tanto al medio ambiente como a _____⁵ mapuche. Jaime comprendió el error de _____⁶ y en una conversación con Andy, renunció a su trabajo con Bartel Aquapower.

la comunidad
insolación
le informó
repuesto
se les pinchó
sus acciones

ᵃse... *he passed out*   ᵇ*would cause*

Nota sobre el lenguaje

If you haven't yet studied the subjunctive mood, here is a quick guide on forming the subjunctive and one of its most common uses.

Forms

To form the present subjunctive, use the "opposite" vowel in verb endings, modeled after the **yo** form of the verb in the present indicative.

tomar: tomo → tom-	=	tom**e**, tom**es**, tom**e**...
volver: vuelvo → vuelv-	=	vuelv**a**, vuelv**as**, vuelv**a**...
pedir: pido → pid-	=	pid**a**, pid**as**, pid**a**...
conocer: conozco → conozc-	=	conozc**a**, conozc**as**, conozc**a**...
decir: digo → dig-	=	dig**a**, dig**as**, dig**a**...

There are also irregular subjunctive forms, such as **dé (dar), esté (estar), vaya (ir), sepa (saber),** and **sea (ser).**

Uses

One of the most common uses of the subjunctive is to express will, desire, or volition (you want someone to do something or you want something to happen). The subjunctive is used because that action exists only in your mind; it hasn't yet happened. Here are a couple of examples.

> **Quiero que me busques** un libro sobre Cervantes.
> *I want you to look for a book on Cervantes for me.*

> **Espero que vengas** a la fiesta el sábado.
> *I hope you come to the party on Saturday.*

You will learn more about the subjunctive throughout your study of Spanish.

A segunda vista

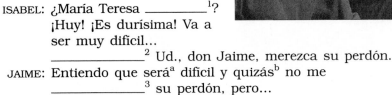

Antes de ver el episodio

Actividad A   ¡A escuchar!

Repasa el siguiente fragmento de la conversación entre doña Isabel, Jaime y don Paco. En unos momentos vas a escuchar la conversación y llenar los espacios en blanco con las palabras correctas. ¡No vuelvas a leer otros fragmentos de este episodio!

> ISABEL: ¿María Teresa _____[1]?
> ¡Huy! ¡Es durísima! Va a
> ser muy difícil...
> _____[2] Ud., don Jaime, merezca su perdón.
> JAIME: Entiendo que será[a] difícil y quizás[b] no me
> _____[3] su perdón, pero...

[a]*it will be*   [b]*perhaps*

Actividad B   El episodio

Ahora vas a ver el episodio de nuevo. Presta atención especial a la escena en que doña Isabel y don Paco hablan con Jaime en la casa y apunta las palabras que faltan para la **Actividad A.** Puedes mirar el episodio más de una vez si quieres.

Después de ver el episodio

Actividad   Intercambio

La familia Sánchez ya sabe que Carlos quiere vender la viña. ¿Por qué crees que quiere venderla si la viña ha tenido tanto éxito? (Recuerda que hace muchos años que Carlos es administrador y que la producción ha sido de muy buena calidad.) ¿Crees que Carlos va a revelar sus intenciones o que va a seguir engañando a la familia? Con un compañero (una compañera) de clase, apunta algunas ideas sobre los posibles motivos de Carlos y lo que crees que va a pasar con él.

EPISODIO 7 ✳ BAJO EL SOL

Detrás de la cámara

You have seen Isabel in a few scenes, and you probably have some idea about the type of person she is. Isabel is compassionate but also strong-willed and cares deeply about her family, the community, and, of course, the winery. After she immigrated with her husband from Spain to Chile, they built a prosperous winery from the ground up. Now an aging widow, Isabel is not in very good health. Despite her frailty, she is not afraid to speak her mind nor is she easily persuaded to do anything against her wishes. In a sense, she is typical of the "strong women" often portrayed by Katherine Hepburn, Bette Davis, and others in the glamour era of the silver screen. Can you think of any other movie characters who are like her?

En el **Episodio 7** Paco menciona el Internet. La imagen que muchas personas tienen de los países hispanos es una de países pobres, del «tercer mundo» y con poca modernización. En general, los países hispanos no gozan de[a] los excesos tecnológicos de una cultura como la de este país, pero no son tan atrasados[b] como algunos creen. España es tan moderna como cualquier otro país de Europa y las ciudades de Santiago, Buenos Aires, Caracas, México, D.F. y San Juan, entre otras, ofrecen casi todo lo que se podría[c] encontrar en las grandes ciudades norteamericanas. Por ejemplo, hay «cibercafés» donde la gente va para tomar un café y leer su correo electrónico. También, los negocios y bancos están tan bien equipados de tecnología como cualquier negocio en este país. Además, la viña donde se filmó *Sol y viento* poseía de[d] todo lo moderno como cualquier viña en Napa o Sonoma, California, por ejemplo. Finalmente, varios Premios Nóbel de Ciencia se han ortogado[e] a científicos de países hispanos. Claro, en las zonas rurales es un poco diferente, pero ¿no es así en casi cualquier país del mundo?

▲ Los cibercafés, como este en México, D.F., son muy populares en todas partes del mundo.

[a]no... *don't enjoy* [b]*backward* [c]se... *one could* [d]poseía... *possessed* [e]*awarded*

Para escribir

Antes de escribir

Paso 1 Hasta ahora sabemos muy poco del pasado de Carlos Sánchez. Para esta actividad, vas a inventar una breve historia en la que describes el pasado de Carlos. Para comenzar, contesta las preguntas a continuación. No hay respuestas correctas; son tus opiniones.

1. ¿Cuántos años tenía Carlos cuando murió su papá? ¿Qué hacía Carlos en esa época? ¿trabajaba? ¿estudiaba? ¿vivía en la viña?

_____

_____

2. Siendo el único hijo varón (*male*), ¿qué responsabilidades, en cuanto a la familia y el manejo (*management*) de la viña, le tocaban a la muerte de su padre?

_____

_____

3. ¿Quería Carlos encargarse de la viña? Si dices que sí, explica por qué era importante para él asumir (*to assume*) este puesto. Si dices que no, ¿qué quería hacer con su vida? ¿Quería casarse? ¿tener hijos? ¿seguir otra profesión? ¿ ?

_____

_____

4. ¿De adolescentes, se llevaban bien Carlos y María? ¿Cómo reaccionó Carlos cuando María decidió trabajar en un campo (*field*) que no fuera (*that wasn't*) la viña?

_____

_____

5. Explica cómo eran las relaciones entre Carlos y Paco tras (*after*) la muerte del padre de Carlos. ¿Lo trataba Paco como si fuera (*as if he were*) su propio hijo? ¿Le ayudaba en los asuntos de la viña? ¿Crees que Carlos respetaba a Paco o que resentía algo de él?

_____

_____

6. Explica las circunstancias que llevaron a Carlos a querer vender la viña. ¿Estaba cansado del trabajo? ¿aburrido? ¿Resentía algo de su familia? ¿Había otros problemas?

_____

_____

 Paso 2 Comparte tu información con un compañero (una compañera) de clase. ¿Tienen Uds. ideas parecidas?

A escribir

Paso 1 Usa tus respuestas de **Antes de ver el episodio** para escribir un borrador en una hoja de papel aparte. Las palabras y expresiones a continuación pueden serte útiles.

además (de)	in addition (to)
al contrario	on the contrary
así que	therefore
creo que	I think that
es obvio/evidente que	it's obvious/evident that
me parece que	it seems to me that
opino que	it's my opinion that
por lo visto	apparently
sin embargo	however

Paso 2 Mira bien lo que has escrito. ¿Quieres agregar palabras, expresiones u oraciones para hacer la narración más interesante?

Paso 3 Intercambia tu composición con la de un compañero (una compañera) de clase para saber sus comentarios. Revisa los siguientes puntos:

☐ el significado y el sentido en general

☐ la concordancia entre sustantivo y adjetivo

☐ la concordancia entre sujeto y verbo

☐ la ortografía

Al entregar la composición

Usa los comentarios de tu compañero/a de clase para escribir una versión final de tu composición. Repasa los siguientes puntos sobre el lenguaje y luego entrégasela a tu profesor(a):

☐ la narración en el pasado (el imperfecto y el pretérito)

☐ el uso del subjuntivo

☐ el uso correcto de palabras de transición

Sin alternativa

Para pensar...

¿Qué lee María cuando Carlos entra en la oficina? ¿Será[a] algo sobre los negocios de su hermano o una carta de Jaime? En otra foto, ¿de qué hablarán don Paco y María?[b] ¿Crees que don Paco trata de convencer a María que haga[c] algo? En la tercera foto, ¿de qué hablarán Carlos y doña Isabel? ¿Con cuál o cuáles de las fotos crees que está relacionado el título del episodio?

[a]*Could it be*   [b]*hablarán... could don Paco and María be talking about*   [c]*que... that she do*

 The Interactive CD-ROM to accompany *Sol y viento* contains additional practice with the story of the film and will help you improve your skills in Spanish.

 The *Sol y viento* Online Learning Center Website contains additional practice materials. Log on to **www.mhhe.com/solyviento**.

SOL Y VIENTO

A primera vista

Antes de ver el episodio

Actividad A ¿Qué recuerdas?

A continuación hay unas citas (*quotes*) de lo que han dicho ciertos personajes en el episodio previo. De los personajes a continuación, ¿puedes indicar quién lo dijo y a quién se lo dijo?

1. «¡El sol está picando fuerte!» _____ se lo dijo a _____.
2. «Ya le dije que esta tierra no se vende.» _____ se lo dijo a _____.
3. «¿Comprende el daño de una represa en la zona?» _____ se lo dijo a _____.
4. «Quizás no me merezca que me perdone.» _____ se lo dijo a _____.
5. «Si pasan cinco días más, no va el negocio.» _____ se lo dijo a _____.

Actividad B Vocabulario útil

Paso 1 Estudia las siguientes palabras y frases.

comprometer	to commit, get involved
confiar en	to trust
cumplir con	to follow through with
las deudas	debts
engañar	to deceive
fracasar	to fail
la inversión	investment
los invitados	guests
renunciar a	to quit
tramposo/a	swindler

Paso 2 Usa las palabras y frases del **Paso 1** para completar cada oración a continuación. **¡OJO!** No se usan todas las palabras y frases.

1. Muchos estudiantes universitarios tienen muchas _____ como la matrícula (*tuition*), el coche o las tarjetas de crédito.
2. Me gustaría _____ mi trabajo porque ya no me gusta nada.
3. ¿A quién quieres _____? Sé que no me dices la verdad.
4. ¿Cuántos _____ vienen a la fiesta?
5. Si no queremos _____ en este proyecto, tenemos que trabajar mucho.

Nota sobre el lenguaje

In Spanish, the present perfect is used to talk about something that *has happened*. If you haven't yet learned the present perfect, use a form of **haber** plus a past participle (**-ado, -ido**). **Haber** is an auxiliary verb that means *to have*, although it is *not* interchangeable with **tener**. It is also irregular in its forms. The first example in the **yo** form means *I have traveled.*

he	hemos	viajado
has	habéis	+ conocido
ha	han	vivido

There are also many irregular past participle forms, a few of which are **dicho (decir)**, **escrito (escribir)**, **hecho (hacer)**, and **visto (ver)**.

The past perfect is used to talk about what *had happened* at a specific point in the past. For the past perfect, use the imperfect of the verb **haber** and a past participle.

Había viajado a Chile antes de tomar este curso.
I had traveled to Chile before taking this course.

Actividad C ¿Qué falta?

En este episodio, Isabel se enfrenta con (*confronts*) Carlos. Lee el diálogo.

ISABEL: ¡Aquí hay más deudas que en todo el tiempo de la administración de tu papá! ¿Qué has hecho con el dinero de «Sol y viento»?

CARLOS: Mamá, estos son tiempos diferentes. El negocio es mucho más difícil.

ISABEL: ¿Me crees tonta? ¿Qué hiciste con el dinero de «Sol y viento»?

CARLOS: _____

¿Qué crees que dice Carlos en el espacio en blanco?

a. Invertí las ganancias (*earnings*) de la viña en varias compañías de tecnología.

b. Me enteré (*I found out*) de que papá había muerto sin pagar muchas de sus deudas y las tuve que pagar yo.

Actividad D El episodio

Ahora mira el episodio. Si hay algo que no entiendes bien, puedes volver a ver la escena en cuestión.

Después de ver el episodio

Actividad A ¿Qué recuerdas?

Contesta las siguientes preguntas sobre el **Episodio 8.**

1. Por fin Carlos le convence a María de que firme los papeles para vender «Sol y viento».
   - **a.** cierto
   - **b.** falso
2. ¿Cuál fue la especialización de Jaime?
   - **a.** economía
   - **b.** ecología
   - **c.** administración de empresas
3. ¿Quién invita a Jaime a la recepción de «Sol y viento»?
   - **a.** don Paco
   - **b.** doña Isabel
4. ¿Qué hizo Carlos con el dinero de «Sol y viento»?
   - **a.** Lo depositó en una cuenta de ahorros en el extranjero.
   - **b.** Lo usó para pagar las deudas de su padre.
   - **c.** Lo invirtió (*he invested*) en compañías de tecnología.

Actividad B ¿Lo captaste?

Verifica tus respuestas de la **Actividad C** en **Antes de ver el episodio.** Si es necesario, puedes ver el episodio de nuevo.

Actividad C Utilizando el contexto

¿Pudiste deducir el significado de las palabras y expresiones que aparecen en letra cursiva a continuación?

YOLANDA: ¿Así vas a estar vestida para la recepción?
MARÍA: No. Me voy a poner un vestido más tarde porque...
YOLANDA: *¡Deja!* Yo me encargo de las flores. *Mejor anda a cambiarte* ahora mismo. ¡Ya van a llegar los invitados!

Actividad D En resumen

Completa la siguiente narración con las palabras y expresiones apropiadas de la lista a la derecha.

En este episodio, María _____[1] que Carlos _____[2] al resto de la familia y a los vecinos. María _____[3] explicaciones a su hermano, pero Carlos _____[4] que sólo él _____[5] el derecho de manejar los negocios de la viña. Luego, María _____[6] a su madre. Entonces doña Isabel _____[7] a su hijo qué _____[8] con el dinero de la viña. Parece que Carlos _____[9] en malas inversiones. A causa de este engaño, doña Isabel _____[10] a su hijo dos opciones.

descubrió
engañaba
había hecho
le dio
le pidió
le preguntó
lo había perdido
respondió
se lo contó todo
tenía

A segunda vista

Antes de ver el episodio

Actividad A ¡A escuchar!

Repasa la siguiente escena. Luego, mientras ves el episodio, completa lo que dicen los personajes con las palabras y expresiones que oyes.

> MARÍA: ¿En serio? ¿Me _____[1] a hablar? ¿Cuándo? Yo creo que ibas a tratar de engañarme... ¡como _____[2] al señor Ayala para sacarle sus terrenos! ¿O acaso no es para eso que está aquí el señor Talavera, para _____[3] y sacarme una firma?
>
> CARLOS: ¿Ese inoportuno?[a] Ni siquiera[b] _____[4] que _____.[5] ¿Y desde cuándo te interesan los negocios de la viña «Sol y viento»? Nunca _____[6] nada. Ni siquiera sabes cómo funciona. ¿Tú crees que esto _____[7] solo?

[a]¿Ese... *That guy?* [b]*even*

Actividad B El episodio

Ahora mira el episodio. No te olvides de hacer la **Actividad A** mientras lo ves. Puedes mirar el episodio más de una vez si quieres.

Después de ver el episodio

Actividad Intercambio

¿Qué piensas de las opciones que le dio doña Isabel a Carlos? ¿Son justas (*fair*) o piensas que hay otra alternativa? ¿Piensas que Carlos va a aceptar las condiciones de su madre o va a rogarle (*beg her*) que él se quede en «Sol y viento»? Con un compañero (una compañera), comenten estas preguntas. Luego, compartan sus ideas con la clase.

Detrás de la cámara

María sometimes feels guilty because she has moved away from home and is not regularly involved in the family business. Yet, when María asks her mother if she wishes that María had stayed at home to work in the vineyard, doña Isabel promptly says "no." Doña Isabel also says that she is proud that her daughter is a university professor. In spite of having moved away, María and her mother maintain a very close relationship, and doña Isabel does not worry at all about María. Although María can be stubborn at times, doña Isabel trusts her daughter, and she knows that María's intelligence and self-confidence serve her well.

SOL Y VIENTO: Enfoque cultural

En el **Episodio 8,** mientras todos se preparan para la recepción, María ayuda a Traimaqueo con algo bastante pesado.ª Él le dice «¡Cuidado!ᵇ ¡Cuidado! Ay, gracias, m'hija.ᶜ» Claro, ya sabes que María no es hija de Traimaqueo. Es muy común entre los hispanohablantes emplear de forma afectuosa los términos **hijo** o **hija** al dirigirseᵈ a una persona más joven. **Tío** y **tía** son utilizados para demostrar cariño a una persona mayor, como lo hace María con don Paco. Paco es amigo de la familia —no es pariente— pero María lo quiere mucho, y por eso le dice **tío Paco.**

En el **Episodio 4** ya viste a Yolanda llamar a Traimaqueo **viejo.** Entre parejas, es frecuente que se llamen **viejo** o **vieja** como muestra de la intimidad y cariño entre ellos. Compara esto con el inglés, en que *my old lady* y *the old man* no son términos tan cariñosos. **Viejo** y **vieja** también se usan entre amigos íntimos y, a veces, entre otros miembros de la familia.

▲ ¿Crees que usa términos de cariño esta pareja tejana (de Texas)?

ª*heavy* ᵇ*Careful!* ᶜ*mi hija* ᵈ*addressing*

Para escribir

Antes de escribir

Paso 1 Para esta actividad, vas a escribir sobre los factores que han contribuido al engaño de Carlos y si piensas que él merece otra oportunidad. Para comenzar, indica si estás de acuerdo o no con las siguientes afirmaciones sobre Carlos.

	ESTOY DE ACUERDO.	NO ESTOY DE ACUERDO.
1. Era muy machista (*male chauvinist*).	☐	☐
2. Sólo pensaba en sí mismo, no en los demás.	☐	☐
3. Se sintió obligado a quedarse a trabajar en la viña después de la muerte de su padre.	☐	☐
4. Invirtió dinero en compañías tecnológicas para su propio beneficio, no por el bien de la viña.	☐	☐
5. Trataba mal a sus empleados (como Traimaqueo) a causa de su propia inseguridad.	☐	☐
6. Le tenía mucha envidia (*envy*) a su hermana María.	☐	☐

	ESTOY DE ACUERDO.	NO ESTOY DE ACUERDO.
7. Pensaba que su madre quería más a María que a él.	☐	☐
8. Invirtió dinero para demostrar (*show*) a su familia que él también era inteligente.	☐	☐
9. Estaba resentido (*resentful*) por el éxito (*success*) profesional de su hermana.	☐	☐

Paso 2 Ahora indica si le darías otra oportunidad a Carlos para quedarse a trabajar en la viña. ¿Qué afirmaciones del **Paso 1** apoyan tu decisión? Piensa en tres argumentos más y escríbelos aquí.

1. _____

2. _____

3. _____

A escribir

Paso 1 Usa tus respuestas de **Antes de ver el episodio** para escribir un borrador en una hoja de papel aparte. Empieza tu composición con una de las siguientes oraciones:

☐ Si fuera (*If I were*) Isabel, le daría (*I would give*) otra oportunidad a Carlos.

☐ Si fuera Isabel, le daría a Carlos las mismas opciones que ella le dio.

Las palabras y expresiones a continuación pueden serte útiles.

además (de)	besides, in addition (to)
(no) lo merece	he deserves (doesn't deserve) it
por eso	that's why, therefore
por fin	finally
sin embargo	however

Paso 2 Mira bien lo que has escrito. ¿Quieres agregar palabras, expresiones u oraciones para hacer la narración más interesante?

Paso 3 Intercambia tu composición con la de un compañero (una compañera) de clase para saber sus comentarios. Revisa los siguientes puntos:

☐ el significado y el sentido en general

☐ la concordancia entre sustantivo y adjetivo

☐ la concordancia entre sujeto y verbo

☐ la ortografía

Al entregar la composición

Usa los comentarios de tu compañero/a de clase para escribir una versión final de tu composición. Repasa los siguientes puntos sobre el lenguaje y luego entrégasela a tu profesor(a):

☐ la narración en el pasado

☐ el uso del subjuntivo

☐ el uso correcto de palabras de transición

Un brindis por el futuro

Para pensar...

Como puedes ver en una de las fotos, doña Isabel se está dirigiendo a[a] los invitados que están presentes para degustar[b] la nueva cosecha. ¿Qué crees que les está diciendo? ¿Saben los invitados de los problemas de «Sol y viento»?

En otra foto, don Paco les habla a doña Isabel y a María. ¿Qué les cuenta? ¿Tiene una solución para salir de las deudas que contrajo[c] Carlos?

En otra foto, Jaime hace una visita al sitio de excavación donde trabaja María. ¿Qué crees que va a pasar? ¿Lo va a perdonar María? ¿Cómo se resuelven los conflictos presentes en la historia de *Sol y viento*?

[a]se... *is addressing* [b]*taste* [c]*acquired*

 The Interactive CD-ROM to accompany *Sol y viento* contains additional practice with the story of the film and will help you improve your skills in Spanish.

 The *Sol y viento* Online Learning Center Website contains additional practice materials. Log on to **www.mhhe.com/solyviento**.

SOL Y VIENTO

A primera vista

Antes de ver el episodio

Actividad A ¿Qué recuerdas?

Contesta cada pregunta con información verdadera, según lo que sabes de *Sol y viento* hasta el momento.

1. ¿Qué palabra describe mejor la actitud de Carlos ante su hermana, María? ¿Está resentido, celoso o enojado Carlos?
2. ¿Cómo supo doña Isabel de los documentos falsificados por Carlos?
3. Jaime dijo que no lo invitaron a la recepción para degustar el vino. ¿Por qué fue, entonces?
4. Cuando doña Isabel confrontó a Carlos en el jardín, le dijo que le quedaban dos opciones. ¿Cuáles eran?
5. Al final del **Episodio 8,** don Paco dijo que María debía escuchar algo. ¿Qué debe escuchar?

Actividad B Vocabulario útil

Paso 1 Estudia las siguientes palabras y frases.

a lo mejor	probably
bienvenido/a	welcome (*adj.*)
hacerse cargo de	to take charge of
humilde	humble

Paso 2 Usa las palabras y frases del **Paso 1** para completar cada oración a continuación.

1. Los buenos amigos son siempre _____ a mi casa.
2. Yo tuve que _____ del asunto porque el señor García era mal administrador.
3. Soy bastante _____. No me gusta hablar de mí mismo.
4. _____ no lo sabes, pero esta mañana hubo un accidente en la oficina.

Nota sobre el lenguaje

If you haven't studied the future tense yet, you can recognize it because all verb forms, whether **-ar** or **-er/-ir,** end with the following: **-ré, -rás, -rá, -remos, -réis, -rán.**

> **tomaré:** *I will take*
>
> **comerán:** *they will eat*
>
> **vivirán:** *they will live*

Some common future verb forms have irregular stems (presented here in the **él/ella** form): **tendrá (tener), hará (hacer), podrá (poder),** and so forth.

Actividad C ¿Qué falta?

Lee la siguiente presentación (*introduction*) y brindis que da doña Isabel al principio del **Episodio 9.** ¿Puedes deducir las palabras y expresiones que faltan?

ISABEL: Señoras y señores: primero que nada, en nombre de mi
_____,¹ quiero agradecer vuestra presencia en esta
importante ocasión. Para la viña «Sol y viento», es un orgullo
que Uds. la visiten. ¡Y espero que el vino que vamos a
degustar esta noche _____² uno de
los mejores que hayan probado en su
vida! También les _____³ presentar
a don Francisco Aguilar, gran amigo
de nuestra familia y apreciado socioª
de la viña «Sol y viento». Él ha venido
desde México a probar nuestro vino.
Bueno, sin más, les quiero _____⁴
nuestra nueva cosecha. ¡Salud!

ª*partner*

Actividad D El episodio

Ahora mira el episodio. **¡OJO!** Sería buena idea *no* mirar todo el episodio y parar al final de la escena en donde degustan el vino. ¡Así guardas la última parte y el fin para **A segunda vista!**

Después de ver el episodio

Actividad A ¿Qué recuerdas?

Contesta cada pregunta según lo que recuerdas del episodio.

1. ¿Qué preguntas hacen los vecinos e invitados? ¿Qué rumores han oído?
2. Don Paco hace un anuncio en público que para la familia implica la salvación de la viña. ¿Qué anuncia él?

Actividad B ¿Lo captaste?

Verifica tus repuestas para la **Actividad C** en **Antes de ver el episodio.** Puedes volver a ver la escena si es necesario.

Actividad C Utilizando el contexto

Utiliza el contexto y la situación para deducir el significado de las expresiones en letra cursiva. Puedes volver a ver esa parte del episodio si quieres.

> INVITADA: Isabel, ¿qué hay de los rumores de que van a vender «Sol y viento»?
>
> INVITADO: Yo también escuché algo así. *¿Qué hay de cierto?*[1]
>
> ISABEL: *Mientras me quede un soplo de vida, ¡no le pasará nada a esta viña ni a estas tierras!*[2] *¡Aquí no se venderá nada!*[3]

1. ...   2. ...   3. ...

Actividad D En resumen

Completa la siguiente narración con las palabras y expresiones apropiadas de la lista a la derecha.

Ya sabes que, antes de comenzar la recepción para degustar el vino de la nueva cosecha de «Sol y viento», don Paco le habla a María. Le _____[1] que escuche a su corazón y que no se guíe solamente _____[2] su cerebro.

    La degustación del vino empieza con una presentación de doña Isabel. _____[3] da a los invitados la bienvenida[a] y luego hace un brindis por la nueva cosecha. Después de probar el vino, algunos vecinos le preguntan sobre algunos rumores que circulan de que _____[4] la viña. Doña Isabel, con aire de mujer decidida, dice: «_____[5] me quede un soplo de vida, no se venderá nada.»

dice
les
mientras
por
se vende

[a]da... *she welcomes the guests*

A segunda vista

Antes de ver el episodio

Actividad A ¡A escuchar!

Repasa la siguiente escena. Luego, mientras ves el episodio, completa lo que dicen los personajes con las palabras y expresiones que oyes.

> MARÍA: ¿Piensa que _____[1] las gracias por ayudar a mi familia?
>
> JAIME: ¡No! En realidad yo _____[2] de otras cosas. Y en todo caso, soy yo el que tiene que _____[3] disculpas por haber causado tantos problemas. Pero la verdad es que yo no _____[4] tú... que Ud.... estaba en medio de todo esto.
>
> MARÍA: ¡Aaah! O sea, si yo no hubiera estado en medio, ¿Ud. habría seguido siendo parte de _____[5] con mi hermano?

Actividad B El episodio

Ahora mira el episodio de nuevo. No te olvides de prestar atención especial a la escena de la **Actividad A** para poder completar el diálogo entre María y Jaime.

Después de ver el episodio

Actividad Intercambio

Ya sabes que hace sólo un día, María no quiso hablar con Jaime. Le dijo a su mamá: «Ese es un nombre que jamás quiero oír de nuevo.» Pero ahora parece que ella perdona a Jaime. ¿A qué crees que se debe este cambio de actitud? Con un compañero (una compañera), comenten este tema. Luego, compartan sus ideas con la clase.

Detrás de la cámara

At the end of the film, Jaime and María reconcile, but not without some difficulty. You already know that María is a very strong-willed person with definite convictions and beliefs. When she found out that Jaime was trying to get Carlos to sell the winery, she took it as a personal offense, thinking that Jaime was using her to get to Carlos. Of course, you know that it was a matter of circumstance that brought Jaime and María together. Or was it? Just as don Paco and doña Isabel conspired to bring Jaime and María together, so too did the forces of nature, as personified by **la machi** and the mystery man who appears throughout the film. Thus, the story concludes with harmony and balance restored to the Earth and to those that inhabit it.

SOL Y VIENTO: Enfoque cultural

En el **Episodio 9** Jaime tiene un problema con el uso de **tú** y **usted.** Acostumbrado a tratar de **tú** (tratamiento de confianza) a María, le cuesta[a] tratarla de **usted** (tratamiento de distancia) después de que ella puso distancia entre ellos, y él quiere decirle que siente mucho lo que ha pasado. Poco después, tiene que preguntarle a María si pueden volver a tutearse.

El uso de **tú** y **usted** en el mundo hispano no es igual de un país a otro. Claro, hay usos que son casi universales, como ocurre cuando un joven se dirige a una mujer mayor de edad, en cuyo[b] caso es indispensable el uso de **usted.** Lo mismo ocurre al dirigirse a una persona de más respetabilidad que la persona que habla, por ejemplo entre estudiantes y profesores: se da el trato de **usted** al profesor, aunque este llame de **tú** al estudiante.

Al hablar de las variaciones en el uso de **tú** frente a **usted,** es de mencionar que en España, por ejemplo, se utiliza **tú** en casos en los que en México y el Perú predomina el uso de **usted.** En algunos países, los miembros de una familia, incluyendo a los abuelos, se tratan de **usted,** mientras que en otras todos los familiares se tutean. Cuando lees algo en español que se dirige al lector, ya sea un artículo o un anuncio, algunas veces verás que se usa **tú,** y en otras, **usted.**

[a]le... *it's hard for him* [b]*whose*

Para escribir

Antes de escribir

Recuerda que la machi comenzó la película narrando una historia, y la voz del narrador nos dice: *She speaks of how the gods seek to keep harmony on the Earth.* Según esta idea, las varias resoluciones, incluyendo las relaciones entre Jaime y María, son manipuladas por los dioses. En esta actividad, vas a escribir sobre la «intervención» de los dioses en las relaciones entre Jaime y María.

Paso 1 Haz una lista de todas las apariciones del «hombre misterioso». ¿Recuerdas quién es? (Es la persona que aparece y desaparece en el **Prólogo.**) Sigue el modelo. Puedes trabajar con un compañero (una compañera) de clase si quieres.

	LUGAR O ESCENA	LO QUE HIZO	CONSECUENCIA
MODELO:	Parque Forestal	Le vendió un papelito de la suerte a Jaime.	Jaime, por estar distraído, chocó con María.

Paso 2 Ahora piensa cómo vas a comenzar tu ensayo. ¿Vas a comenzarlo con una pregunta? ¿con una oración? Compara los siguientes comienzos para estimular tus ideas.

MODELOS: ¿Ha pensado Ud. alguna vez si lo que le pasa se debe solamente al destino, no al libre albedrío (*free will*)? ¿Hay «otro mundo» que nos observa y que asegura (*makes sure*) que todo resulte de una u otra manera? Esta es la premisa de *Sol y viento*.

Desde épocas remotas el hombre siempre ha creído en algo llamado «el destino». Predeterminado por un plan divino o por otra(s) fuerza(s), uno no crea su destino; el destino le toca. Esta es la premisa de *Sol y viento*.

A escribir

Paso 1 Usa las ideas de **Antes de escribir** para escribir un borrador en una hoja de papel aparte.

Paso 2 Mira bien lo que has escrito. ¿Quieres agregar palabras, expresiones u oraciones para hacer la narración más interesante?

 Paso 3 Intercambia tu composición con la de un compañero (una compañera) de clase para saber sus comentarios. Revisa los siguientes puntos:

☐ el significado y el sentido en general
☐ la concordancia entre sustantivo y adjetivo
☐ la concordancia entre sujeto y verbo
☐ la ortografía

Al entregar la composición

Usa los comentarios de tu compañero/a de clase para escribir una versión final de tu narración. Repasa los siguientes puntos sobre el lenguaje y luego entrégasela a tu profesor(a):

☐ la narración en el pasado
☐ el uso correcto del subjuntivo
☐ el uso correcto del futuro
☐ el uso correcto de palabras de transición

ANSWER KEY

Prólogo

Antes de ver el episodio
Actividad B (*Actual answers*) *María:* 1. *false* 2. *false* 3. *true* *Jaime:* 1. *true* 2. *false* 3. *true* **Actividad C** a
Después de ver el episodio
Actividad A 1. c 2. b 3. b 4. c **Actividad C** *pretty*

Episodio 1

A primera vista
Antes de ver el episodio
Actividad A 1. *false* 2. *true* 3. *true* 4. *true* 5. *true* **Actividad B Paso 2** 1. Para servirlo 2. ¿Qué se le ofrece? 3. ¡Claro que sí!
4. A propósito **Actividad C Paso 1** 1. c 2. b
Después de ver el episodio
Actividad A 1. Sí 2. Hotel Bonaparte 3. Maipo 4. Talavera, Verdejo 5. b 6. a **Actividad C Paso 1** *How much will it be? / Is that okay?* **Paso 2** *Let's go.*

A segunda vista
Antes de ver el episodio
Actividad A 1. la viña 2. con 3. Soy 4. que 5. estoy 6. como 7. Muy bien 8. espero 9. Hasta

Episodio 2

A primera vista
Antes de ver el episodio
Actividad A 1. falso 2. cierto 3. falso 4. cierto 5. falso **Actividad B Paso 2** 1. ¡Qué coincidencia! 2. Ojalá que nos veamos de nuevo 3. ¡Espere! **Actividad C** 1. b 2. a 3. c 4. a
Después de ver el episodio
Actividad A 1. b 2. c 3. c 4. b 5. a 6. b **Actividad C** *I was distracted; (he) was reading*
Actividad D 1. corre 2. vende 3. lee 4. se choca con 5. decide 6. espera 7. hablan 8. necesita

A segunda vista
Antes de ver el episodio
Actividad A 1. Tres 2. Tres 3. trescientos 4. Esa 5. esa 6. esa 7. trescientos 8. estos

Episodio 3

A primera vista
Antes de ver el episodio
Actividad A 1. falso 2. cierto 3. cierto 4. cierto 5. falso **Actividad B Paso 2** 1. f 2. a 3. d 4. e 5. c 6. b **Actividad C** 1. b 2. c 3. b
Después de ver el episodio
Actividad A 1. b 2. a 3. a 4. a 5. a 6. a **Actividad C** Traimaqueo lo puede guiar: lo = a Ud. (Jaime); Yo lo voy a llamar… : lo = a él (Traimaqueo) **Actividad D** 1. conoce 2. toman 3. hablan 4. venta 5. quiere 6. tiene 7. insiste 8. contrato

A segunda vista
Antes de ver el episodio
Actividad A 1. bodega 2. vino 3. vino chileno 4. prefiero 6. importantes 6. oficina

Episodio 4

A primera vista
Antes de ver el episodio
Actividad A 1. Jaime 2. María 3. Mario, Carlos 4. la madre de Carlos, Carlos **Actividad B Paso 2** 1. regalo 2. cepas 3. Nací, me enterrarán 4. se equivocan 5. topacio **Actividad C** b
Después de ver el episodio
Actividad A 1. Traimaqueo. Mario no los acompañó. 2. no 3. No, no le dijo la verdad. 4. para María **Actividad C** 1. *Is that okay with you?* 2. *How much is it? / I'll take it.* **Actividad D** 1. conoce 2. poema 3. pasión 4. madre 5. agradable 6. pueblo mapuche 7. espíritu

A segunda vista
Antes de ver el episodio
Actividad A 1. profesora 2. para 3. lindo 4. tarjeta

Episodio 5

A primera vista
Antes de ver el episodio
Actividad A 1. falso 2. cierto 3. cierto 4. falso 5. falso **Actividad B Paso 2** 1. Los campesinos 2. La Bolsa (de valores) 3. Te encargaste de 4. Brindemos 5. Vamos a tutearnos **Actividad C** 1. b 2. b 3. a
Después de ver el episodio
Actividad A 1. b 2. a 3. Habló con su esposo que ya murió. 4. «gente de la tierra» 5. b 6. b 7. b **Actividad C** 1. no van bien 2. quiere vender 3. no le gusta nada 4. pasan 5. le parece que 6. le cuenta 7. van bien 8. le da

A segunda vista
Antes de ver el episodio
Actividad A 1. quedé 2. pasa 3. pasa 4. conozco 5. tengo 6. murió 7. encargaste 8. estaba 9. tenía

Episodio 6

A primera vista
Antes de ver el episodio
Actividad A 1. cierto 2. falso 3. falso 4. cierto 5. cierto **Actividad B Paso 2** 1. jitomates 2. ¿Qué tal están? 3. ¡Pruébelos!
4. Déme **Actividad C** 1. a 2. b
Después de ver el episodio
Actividad A 1. b 2. a 3. b 4. b 5. b **Actividad C Paso 1** *How fresh/good are . . . ?* **Paso 2** «Aló» / «Diga» **Actividad D** 1. está
preocupada 2. le cae bien 3. lo respeta 4. conoce a 5. está a la venta 6. aeropuerto 7. el amuleto

A segunda vista
Antes de ver el episodio
Actividad A 1. Nos 2. tampoco 3. tierras 4. espere 5. necesaria 6. le dije 7. hermana 8. he visto 9. importa

Episodio 7

A primera vista
Antes de ver el episodio
Actividad A 1. falso 2. cierto 3. cierto 4. cierto 5. falso **Actividad B Paso 2** 1. represa 2. ruedas 3. atraviesa por 4. el repuesto
5. los hechos **Actividad C** 1. b 2. b
Después de ver el episodio
Actividad A 1. c 2. a 3. c 4. a 5. b **Actividad C** 1. se les pinchó 2. repuesto 3. insolación 4. le informó 5. la comunidad
6. sus acciones

A segunda vista
Antes de ver el episodio
Actividad A 1. perdonar 2. A menos que 3. merezca

Episodio 8

A primera vista
Antes de ver el episodio
Actividad A 1. Mario, Jaime 2. doña Isabel, Jaime 3. don Paco, Jaime 4. Jaime, doña Isabel 5. Jaime, don Paco y doña
Isabel. **Actividad B Paso 2** 1. deudas 2. renunciar a 3. engañar 4. invitados 5. fracasar
Actividad C a
Después de ver el episodio
Actividad A 1. b 2. c 3. a 4. c **Actividad C** *Stop!, You should go change* **Actividad D** 1. descubrió 2. engañaba 3. le pidió
4. respondió 5. tenía 6. se lo contó todo 7. le preguntó 8. había hecho 9. lo había perdido 10. le dio

A segunda vista
Antes de ver el episodio
Actividad A 1. ibas 2. engañaste 3. seducirme 4. sabía 5. se conocían 6. has hecho 7. se maneja

Episodio 9

A primera vista
Antes de ver el episodio
Actividad A 1. resentido 2. María se lo dijo. 3. Porque don Paco lo invitó. 4. Ella puede llamar a las autoridades o él puede renunciar a su conexión con la viña y desaparecer. 5. su corazón **Actividad B Paso 2** 1. bienvenidos 2. hacerme cargo 3. humilde 4. A lo mejor **Actividad C** 1. familia 2. sea 3. quiero 4. presentar
Después de ver el episodio
Actividad A 1. Han oído rumores de la venta de «Sol y viento». 2. Que tienen un acuerdo con un distribuidor y van a expandir las exportaciones a Norteamérica. **Actividad C** 1. *What's really going on?* 2. *As long as I still live, nothing will happen to this vineyard or to this land!* 3. *Nothing will be sold here!* **Actividad D** 1. dice 2. por 3. Les 4. se vende 5. Mientras

A segunda vista
Antes de ver el episodio
Actividad A 1. debo darle 2. quería hablar 3. pedir 4. sabía que 5. ese negocio

VERBS

A. Regular Verbs: Simple Tenses

INFINITIVE PRESENT PARTICIPLE PAST PARTICIPLE	INDICATIVE					SUBJUNCTIVE		IMPERATIVE
	PRESENT	IMPERFECT	PRETERITE	FUTURE	CONDITIONAL	PRESENT	IMPERFECT	
hablar hablando hablado	hablo hablas habla hablamos habláis hablan	hablaba hablabas hablaba hablábamos hablabais hablaban	hablé hablaste habló hablamos hablasteis hablaron	hablaré hablarás hablará hablaremos hablaréis hablarán	hablaría hablarías hablaría hablaríamos hablaríais hablarían	hable hables hable hablemos habléis hablen	hablara hablaras hablara habláramos hablarais hablaran	habla / no hables hable hablemos hablad / no habléis hablen
comer comiendo comido	como comes come comemos coméis comen	comía comías comía comíamos comíais comían	comí comiste comió comimos comisteis comieron	comeré comerás comerá comeremos comeréis comerán	comería comerías comería comeríamos comeríais comerían	coma comas coma comamos comáis coman	comiera comieras comiera comiéramos comierais comieran	come / no comas coma comamos comed / no comáis coman
vivir viviendo vivido	vivo vives vive vivimos vivís viven	vivía vivías vivía vivíamos vivíais vivían	viví viviste vivió vivimos vivisteis vivieron	viviré vivirás vivirá viviremos viviréis vivirán	viviría vivirías viviría viviríamos viviríais vivirían	viva vivas viva vivamos viváis vivan	viviera vivieras viviera viviéramos vivierais vivieran	vive / no vivas viva vivamos vivid / no viváis vivan

B. Regular Verbs: Perfect Tenses

INDICATIVE								SUBJUNCTIVE			
PRESENT PERFECT		PAST PERFECT		PRETERITE PERFECT		FUTURE PERFECT		CONDITIONAL PERFECT		PRESENT PERFECT		PAST PERFECT	
he has ha hemos habéis han	hablado comido vivido	había habías había habíamos habíais habían	hablado comido vivido	hube hubiste hubo hubimos hubisteis hubieron	hablado comido vivido	habré habrás habrá habremos habréis habrán	hablado comido vivido	habría habrías habría habríamos habríais habrían	hablado comido vivido	haya hayas haya hayamos hayáis hayan	hablado comido vivido	hubiera hubieras hubiera hubiéramos hubierais hubieran	hablado comido vivido

C. Irregular Verbs

INFINITIVE PRESENT PARTICIPLE PAST PARTICIPLE	INDICATIVE					SUBJUNCTIVE		IMPERATIVE
	PRESENT	IMPERFECT	PRETERITE	FUTURE	CONDITIONAL	PRESENT	IMPERFECT	
andar andando andado	ando andas anda andamos andáis andan	andaba andabas andaba andábamos andabais andaban	anduve anduviste anduvo anduvimos anduvisteis anduvieron	andaré andarás andará andaremos andaréis andarán	andaría andarías andaría andaríamos andaríais andarían	ande andes ande andemos andéis anden	anduviera anduvieras anduviera anduviéramos anduvierais anduvieran	anda / no andes ande andemos andad / no andéis anden
caer cayendo caído	caigo caes cae caemos caéis caen	caía caías caía caíamos caíais caían	caí caíste cayó caímos caísteis cayeron	caeré caerás caerá caeremos caeréis caerán	caería caerías caería caeríamos caeríais caerían	caiga caigas caiga caigamos caigáis caigan	cayera cayeras cayera cayéramos cayerais cayeran	cae / no caigas caiga caigamos caed / no caigáis caigan
dar dando dado	doy das da damos dais dan	daba dabas daba dábamos dabais daban	di diste dio dimos disteis dieron	daré darás dará daremos daréis darán	daría darías daría daríamos daríais darían	dé des dé demos deis den	diera dieras diera diéramos dierais dieran	da / no des dé demos dad / no deis den
decir diciendo dicho	digo dices dice decimos decís dicen	decía decías decía decíamos decíais decían	dije dijiste dijo dijimos dijisteis dijeron	diré dirás dirá diremos diréis dirán	diría dirías diría diríamos diríais dirían	diga digas diga digamos digáis digan	dijera dijeras dijera dijéramos dijerais dijeran	di / no digas diga digamos decid / no digáis digan
estar estando estado	estoy estás está estamos estáis están	estaba estabas estaba estábamos estabais estaban	estuve estuviste estuvo estuvimos estuvisteis estuvieron	estaré estarás estará estaremos estaréis estarán	estaría estarías estaría estaríamos estaríais estarían	esté estés esté estemos estéis estén	estuviera estuvieras estuviera estuviéramos estuvierais estuvieran	está / no estés esté estemos estad / no estéis estén
haber habiendo habido	he has ha hemos habéis han	había habías había habíamos habíais habían	hube hubiste hubo hubimos hubisteis hubieron	habré habrás habrá habremos habréis habrán	habría habrías habría habríamos habríais habrían	haya hayas haya hayamos hayáis hayan	hubiera hubieras hubiera hubiéramos hubierais hubieran	
hacer haciendo hecho	hago haces hace hacemos hacéis hacen	hacía hacías hacía hacíamos hacíais hacían	hice hiciste hizo hicimos hicisteis hicieron	haré harás hará haremos haréis harán	haría harías haría haríamos haríais harían	haga hagas haga hagamos hagáis hagan	hiciera hicieras hiciera hiciéramos hicierais hicieran	haz / no hagas haga hagamos haced / no hagáis hagan

C. Irregular Verbs (continued)

INFINITIVE PRESENT PARTICIPLE PAST PARTICIPLE	INDICATIVE					SUBJUNCTIVE		IMPERATIVE
	PRESENT	IMPERFECT	PRETERITE	FUTURE	CONDITIONAL	PRESENT	IMPERFECT	
ir yendo ido	voy vas va vamos vais van	iba ibas iba íbamos ibais iban	fui fuiste fue fuimos fuisteis fueron	iré irás irá iremos iréis irán	iría irías iría iríamos iríais irían	vaya vayas vaya vayamos vayáis vayan	fuera fueras fuera fuéramos fuerais fueran	ve / no vayas vaya vamos / no vayamos id / no vayáis vayan
oír oyendo oído	oigo oyes oye oímos oís oyen	oía oías oía oíamos oíais oían	oí oíste oyó oímos oísteis oyeron	oiré oirás oirá oiremos oiréis oirán	oiría oirías oiría oiríamos oiríais oirían	oiga oigas oiga oigamos oigáis oigan	oyera oyeras oyera oyéramos oyerais oyeran	oye / no oigas oiga oigamos oíd / no oigáis oigan
poder pudiendo podido	puedo puedes puede podemos podéis pueden	podía podías podía podíamos podíais podían	pude pudiste pudo pudimos pudisteis pudieron	podré podrás podrá podremos podréis podrán	podría podrías podría podríamos podríais podrían	pueda puedas pueda podamos podáis puedan	pudiera pudieras pudiera pudiéramos pudierais pudieran	
poner poniendo puesto	pongo pones pone ponemos ponéis ponen	ponía ponías ponía poníamos poníais ponían	puse pusiste puso pusimos pusisteis pusieron	pondré pondrás pondrá pondremos pondréis pondrán	pondría pondrías pondría pondríamos pondríais pondrían	ponga pongas ponga pongamos pongáis pongan	pusiera pusieras pusiera pusiéramos pusierais pusieran	pon / no pongas ponga pongamos poned / no pongáis pongan
querer queriendo querido	quiero quieres quiere queremos queréis quieren	quería querías quería queríamos queríais querían	quise quisiste quiso quisimos quisisteis quisieron	querré querrás querrá querremos querréis querrán	querría querrías querría querríamos querríais querrían	quiera quieras quiera queramos queráis quieran	quisiera quisieras quisiera quisiéramos quisierais quisieran	quiere / no quieras quiera queramos quered / no queráis quieran
saber sabiendo sabido	sé sabes sabe sabemos sabéis saben	sabía sabías sabía sabíamos sabíais sabían	supe supiste supo supimos supisteis supieron	sabré sabrás sabrá sabremos sabréis sabrán	sabría sabrías sabría sabríamos sabríais sabrían	sepa sepas sepa sepamos sepáis sepan	supiera supieras supiera supiéramos supierais supieran	sabe / no sepas sepa sepamos sabed / no sepáis sepan
salir saliendo salido	salgo sales sale salimos salís salen	salía salías salía salíamos salíais salían	salí saliste salió salimos salisteis salieron	saldré saldrás saldrá saldremos saldréis saldrán	saldría saldrías saldría saldríamos saldríais saldrían	salga salgas salga salgamos salgáis salgan	saliera salieras saliera saliéramos salierais salieran	sal / no salgas salga salgamos salid / no salgáis salgan

C. Irregular Verbs (*continued*)

INFINITIVE PRESENT PARTICIPLE PAST PARTICIPLE	INDICATIVE					SUBJUNCTIVE		IMPERATIVE
	PRESENT	IMPERFECT	PRETERITE	FUTURE	CONDITIONAL	PRESENT	IMPERFECT	
ser siendo sido	soy eres es somos sois son	era eras era éramos erais eran	fui fuiste fue fuimos fuisteis fueron	seré serás será seremos seréis serán	sería serías sería seríamos seríais serían	sea seas sea seamos seáis sean	fuera fueras fuera fuéramos fuerais fueran	sé / no seas sea seamos sed / no seáis sean
tener teniendo tenido	tengo tienes tiene tenemos tenéis tienen	tenía tenías tenía teníamos teníais tenían	tuve tuviste tuvo tuvimos tuvisteis tuvieron	tendré tendrás tendrá tendremos tendréis tendrán	tendría tendrías tendría tendríamos tendríais tendrían	tenga tengas tenga tengamos tengáis tengan	tuviera tuvieras tuviera tuviéramos tuvierais tuvieran	ten / no tengas tenga tengamos tened / no tengáis tengan
traer trayendo traído	traigo traes trae traemos traéis traen	traía traías traía traíamos traíais traían	traje trajiste trajo trajimos trajisteis trajeron	traeré traerás traerá traeremos traeréis traerán	traería traerías traería traeríamos traeríais traerían	traiga traigas traiga traigamos traigáis traigan	trajera trajeras trajera trajéramos trajerais trajeran	trae / no traigas traiga traigamos traed / no traigáis traigan
venir viniendo venido	vengo vienes viene venimos venís vienen	venía venías venía veníamos veníais venían	vine viniste vino vinimos vinisteis vinieron	vendré vendrás vendrá vendremos vendréis vendrán	vendría vendrías vendría vendríamos vendríais vendrían	venga vengas venga vengamos vengáis vengan	viniera vinieras viniera viniéramos vinierais vinieran	ven / no vengas venga vengamos venid / no vengáis vengan
ver viendo visto	veo ves ve vemos veis ven	veía veías veía veíamos veíais veían	vi viste vio vimos visteis vieron	veré verás verá veremos veréis verán	vería verías vería veríamos veríais verían	vea veas vea veamos veáis vean	viera vieras viera viéramos vierais vieran	ve / no veas vea veamos ved / no veáis vean

D. Stem-Changing and Spelling Change Verbs

INFINITIVE PRESENT PARTICIPLE PAST PARTICIPLE	INDICATIVE					SUBJUNCTIVE		IMPERATIVE
	PRESENT	IMPERFECT	PRETERITE	FUTURE	CONDITIONAL	PRESENT	IMPERFECT	
construir (y) construyendo construido	construyo construyes construye construimos construís construyen	construía construías construía construíamos construíais construían	construí construiste construyó construimos construisteis construyeron	construiré construirás construirá construiremos construiréis construirán	construiría construirías construiría construiríamos construiríais construirían	construya construyas construya construyamos construyáis construyan	construyera construyeras construyera construyéramos construyerais construyeran	construye / no construyas construya construyamos construid / no construyáis construyan
dormir (ue, u) durmiendo dormido	duermo duermes duerme dormimos dormís duermen	dormía dormías dormía dormíamos dormíais dormían	dormí dormiste durmió dormimos dormisteis durmieron	dormiré dormirás dormirá dormiremos dormiréis dormirán	dormiría dormirías dormiría dormiríamos dormiríais dormirían	duerma duermas duerma durmamos durmáis duerman	durmiera durmieras durmiera durmiéramos durmierais durmieran	duerme / no duermas duerma durmamos dormid / no durmáis duerman

D. Stem-Changing and Spelling Change Verbs (*continued*)

INFINITIVE PRESENT PARTICIPLE PAST PARTICIPLE	INDICATIVE					SUBJUNCTIVE		IMPERATIVE
	PRESENT	IMPERFECT	PRETERITE	FUTURE	CONDITIONAL	PRESENT	IMPERFECT	
pedir (i, i) pidiendo pedido	pido pides pide pedimos pedís piden	pedía pedías pedía pedíamos pedíais pedían	pedí pediste pidió pedimos pedisteis pidieron	pediré pedirás pedirá pediremos pediréis pedirán	pediría pedirías pediría pediríamos pediríais pedirían	pida pidas pida pidamos pidáis pidan	pidiera pidieras pidiera pidiéramos pidierais pidieran	pide / no pidas pida pidamos pedid / no pidáis pidan
pensar (ie) pensando pensado	pienso piensas piensa pensamos pensáis piensan	pensaba pensabas pensaba pensábamos pensabais pensaban	pensé pensaste pensó pensamos pensasteis pensaron	pensaré pensarás pensará pensaremos pensaréis pensarán	pensaría pensarías pensaría pensaríamos pensaríais pensarían	piense pienses piense pensemos penséis piensen	pensara pensaras pensara pensáramos pensarais pensaran	piensa / no pienses piense pensemos pensad / no penséis piensen
producir (zc) produciendo producido	produzco produces produce producimos producís producen	producía producías producía producíamos producíais producían	produje produjiste produjo produjimos produjisteis produjeron	produciré producirás producirá produciremos produciréis producirán	produciría producirías produciría produciríamos produciríais producirían	produzca produzcas produzca produzcamos produzcáis produzcan	produjera produjeras produjera produjéramos produjerais produjeran	produce / no produzcas produzca produzcamos producid / no produzcáis produzcan
reír (i, i) riendo reído	río ríes ríe reímos reís ríen	reía reías reía reíamos reíais reían	reí reíste rió reímos reísteis rieron	reiré reirás reirá reiremos reiréis reirán	reiría reirías reiría reiríamos reiríais reirían	ría rías ría riamos riáis rían	riera rieras riera riéramos rierais rieran	ríe / no rías ría riamos reíd / no riáis rían
seguir (i, i) (g) siguiendo seguido	sigo sigues sigue seguimos seguís siguen	seguía seguías seguía seguíamos seguíais seguían	seguí seguiste siguió seguimos seguisteis siguieron	seguiré seguirás seguirá seguiremos seguiréis seguirán	seguiría seguirías seguiría seguiríamos seguiríais seguirían	siga sigas siga sigamos sigáis sigan	siguiera siguieras siguiera siguiéramos siguierais siguieran	sigue / no sigas siga sigamos seguid / no sigáis sigan
sentir (ie, i) sintiendo sentido	siento sientes siente sentimos sentís sienten	sentía sentías sentía sentíamos sentíais sentían	sentí sentiste sintió sentimos sentisteis sintieron	sentiré sentirás sentirá sentiremos sentiréis sentirán	sentiría sentirías sentiría sentiríamos sentiríais sentirían	sienta sientas sienta sintamos sintáis sientan	sintiera sintieras sintiera sintiéramos sintierais sintieran	siente / no sientas sienta sintamos sentid / no sintáis sientan
volver (ue) volviendo vuelto	vuelvo vuelves vuelve volvemos volvéis vuelven	volvía volvías volvía volvíamos volvíais volvían	volví volviste volvió volvimos volvisteis volvieron	volveré volverás volverá volveremos volveréis volverán	volvería volverías volvería volveríamos volveríais volverían	vuelva vuelvas vuelva volvamos volváis vuelvan	volviera volvieras volviera volviéramos volvierais volvieran	vuelve / no vuelvas vuelva volvamos volved / no volváis vuelvan

SPANISH-ENGLISH VOCABULARY

This Spanish-English Vocabulary contains all the words that appear in the text and other components of *Sol y viento,* including the film and CD-ROM, with the following exceptions: (1) most identical cognates that do not appear in the chapter vocabulary lists; (2) verb forms; (3) diminutives in **-ito/a;** (4) absolute superlatives in **-ísimo/a;** and (5) most adverbs in **-mente.** Active vocabulary is listed for the *Sol y viento* main text and is indicated by the number of the lesson in which a word or given meaning is first listed (P = **Lección preliminar**). Vocabulary that is glossed in the text is not considered to be active vocabulary, and no lesson number is indicated for it. Only meanings that are used in this program are given.

Gender is indicated except for masculine nouns ending in **-o,** feminine nouns ending in -**a,** and invariable adjectives. Stem changes and spelling changes are indicated for verbs: **dormir (ue, u); llegar (gu).**

Because **ch** and **ll** are no longer considered separate letters, words with **ch** and **ll** are alphabetized as they would be in English. The letter **ñ** follows the letter **n: añadir** follows **anuncio,** for example.

The following abbreviations are used:

adj.	adjective	*m.*	masculine
adv.	adverb	*Mex.*	Mexico
Arg.	Argentina	*n.*	noun
aux.	auxiliary	*neut.*	neuter
conj.	conjunction	*obj.*	object
def. art.	definite article	*p.p.*	past participle
d.o.	direct object	*pl.*	plural
f.	feminine	*poss.*	possessive
fam.	familiar	*prep.*	preposition
form.	formal	*pron.*	pronoun
gram.	grammatical term	*refl.*	reflexive
indef. art.	indefinite article	*s.*	singular
inf.	infinitive	*Sp.*	Spain
inv.	invariable	*sub. pron.*	subject pronoun
i.o.	indirect object	*v.*	verb
irreg.	irregular		

A

a to, at (1B); **a continuación** following; **a la derecha de** to the right of (2A); **a la izquierda de** to the left of (2A); **a la misma hora** at the same time (1A); **a la(s)…** at … o'clock (1A); **¿a qué hora?** at what time? (1A); **a solas** alone (1B); **llegar (gu) a tiempo** to arrive on time (1A)

abajo below, underneath

abierto/a (*p.p. of* **abrir**) open

abogado/a lawyer (9B)

abogar (gu) por to advocate

abordar to board

aborto abortion

abrazar (c) to embrace (7B)

abrigo overcoat (2B)

abril *m.* April (1B)

abrir (*p.p.* **abierto/a**) to open (1B)

abrochar(se) (el cinturón) to fasten (one's seatbelt)

absoluto/a absolute; complete

abstención *f.* abstention

abstracto/a abstract

abuelo/a grandfather, grandmother (3A); *pl.* grandparents

aburrido/a bored (1B); boring (2B)

aburrir(se) to bore (oneself) (7A)

abusar de to abuse (*someone*) (9A)

acá here

acabar to finish; **acabar de** + *inf.* to have just (*done something*)

academia academy

académico/a academic

acampar to camp (6B)

acaparado/a monopolized

acariciar to caress (7B)

acaso: por si acaso just in case

acceder a to consent to

acceso access

accesorio accessory

accidente *m.* accident (8B)

acción *f.* action; **Día** (*m.*) **de Acción de Gracias** Thanksgiving (4A); *pl.* stocks (8A)

aceite *m.* oil; **aceite de oliva** olive oil

aceptable acceptable

aceptación *f.* acceptance

aceptar to accept

acerca de about

acero steel (8A)

acertar (ie) to guess right

ácido acid

aclaración *f.* clarification

acomodar to settle; to make comfortable

acompañar to accompany; to go with

acondicionado: aire (*m.*) **acondicionado** air conditioning

aconsejar to advise (9A)

acontecimiento event, happening (8B)

acostarse (ue) to go to bed (2A)

acostumbrarse a to get used to, to become accustomed to

actitud *f.* attitude

actividad *f.* activity

activista *m., f.* activist

activo/a active

acto act

actor *m.* actor (9B)

actriz *f.* (*pl.* **actrices**) actress (9B)

actual current; contemporary

actualidad *f.*: **en la actualidad** currently

actuar (actúo) to act

acuario Aquarius

acuático/a aquatic

acuerdo agreement; **estar** (*irreg.*) **de acuerdo** to agree; **ponerse** (*irreg.*) **de acuerdo** to come to an agreement

adaptable adaptable (5A)

adaptarse to adapt

adecuado/a appropriate

adelante *adv.* ahead

además moreover; **además de** besides

adentro *adv.* inside

adicional additional

adiós good-bye

adivinar to guess

adjetivo adjective

administración *f.* administration; **administración de empresas** business administration (P)

administrador(a) administrator

admirador(a) fan, admirer

admirar to admire

adolescencia adolescence

adolescente *m., f.* adolescent, teenager (5A)

¿adónde? where (to)? (1B)

adoptar to adopt

adoptivo/a adopted (3A)

adorar to adore, worship (7B)

adquirido/a acquired; **síndrome** (*m.*) **de inmunodeficiencia adquirida (SIDA)** Acquired Immune Deficiency Syndrome (AIDS) (8B)

adquisición *f.* acquisition

aduana *s.* customs; **pasar por la aduana** to go through customs (6A)

adulto/a adult; **edad** (*f.*) **adulta** adulthood

adverbio adverb

advertir (ie, i) (de) to warn (about)

aéreo/a: línea aérea airline

aeróbico aerobic; **hacer** (*irreg.*) **ejercico aeróbico** to do aerobics (4A)

aeropuerto airport (6A)

afán *m.* desire

afectar to affect (7A)

afectuoso/a affectionate

afeitarse to shave (5A)

aficionado/a fan; **ser** (*irreg.*) **aficionado/a (a)** to be a fan (of) (4A)

afirmación *f.* statement

afirmar to affirm

afirmativo/a *adj.* affirmative

afluencia throng, horde

afortunadamente fortunately, luckily

África Africa (6B)

africano/a *n., adj.* African

afroamericano/a *n., adj.* African-American

afuera *adv.* outside; *n. pl.* suburbs, outskirts (2A)

agencia agency; **agencia de viajes** travel agency (6A)

agenda electrónica electronic organizer, PDA (personal digital assistant) (5A)

agente *m., f.* agent; **agente de inmobilaria** real estate agent; **agente de viajes** travel agent (6A)

agitado/a agitated, shaken

agosto August (1B)

agradable pleasant, nice (1B)

agradar to please (5A)

agradecer (zc) to thank (3A)

agradecido/a thankful (9A)

agregar (gu) to add

agrícola *adj. m., f.* agricultural (8A)

agrio/a sour (3B)

agrupación *f.* group

agrupar to group

agua *f.* (*but* **el agua**) water (3B); **agua corriente** running water; **agua del grifo** tap water; **agua potable** drinking water; **contaminación** (*f.*) **del agua** water pollution (6B); **esquiar (esquío) en el agua** to water ski (4A)

aguacate *m.* avocado (3B)

aguado/a watered down

aguafiestas *m., f. s.* party-pooper (4A)

aguantar to endure; **no aguantar** not to be able to stand, put up with (7B)

ahí there

ahora now (1A)

ahorrar to save (8A)

ahorros *pl.* savings (8A); **cuenta de ahorros** savings account (8A)

aimará *m.* Aimara (language)

aire *m.* air; **aire acondicionado** air conditioning; **al aire libre** outdoors (6B); **contaminación** (*f.*) **del aire** air pollution (6B)

aislado/a isolated

ajedrez *m.* chess (4A)

ajeno/a foreign

ajo garlic

al (*contraction of* **a** + **el**) to the; **al aire libre** outdoors (6B); **al este de** to the east of (2A); **al horno** baked (3B); **al igual que** just like; **al lado de** beside (2A); **al norte de** to the north of (2A); **al oeste de** to the west of (2A); **al sur de** to the south of (2A); **al vapor** steamed (3B)

alarma *m.* alarm

alarmante alarming

alberca (*Mex.*) swimming pool

alcachofa artichoke

alcanzar (c) (una meta) to reach, achieve (a goal) (9B)

alcoba bedroom

alcohol *m.* alcohol

alcohólico/a *adj.* alcoholic; **bebida alcohólica** alcoholic drink

alegrarse to get, become happy (7A)

alegre happy (1B)

alegría happiness

alemán *m.* German (*language*) (P)

alergia allergy (7A)

alérgico/a allergic

alfombra rug; carpet (4B)

algo something, some (3B)

algodón *m.* cotton (2B)

alguien someone (1B)

algún, alguno/a some, any (3B)

alianza alliance

aliento breath; **mal aliento** bad breath

alimenticio/a nutritional

alimento food item (3B)

aliviar to alleviate

allá (way) over there

allí there (2B); over there (2B)

almacén *m.* department store (2A)

almendrado/a almond-shaped

almohada pillow

almorzar (ue) (c) to eat lunch (2A)

almuerzo lunch (3B)

alojamiento lodging (6A)

alojarse to stay (*in a place*) (6A)

alpinismo rock climbing; **practicar (qu) el alpinismo de rocas** to rock climb (6B)

alquilar to rent (4B); **se alquila** for rent (4B)

alquiler *m.* rent (1A)

alrededor de *prep.* around (2A)

alternativa *n.* alternative, choice

alterno/a alternating

alto/a tall (3A); high; **en voz alta** aloud; **zapatos de tacón alto** high-heeled shoes (2B)

altruista *adj. m., f.* altruistic
altura height
alubia bean
aluminio aluminum; **lata de aluminio** aluminum can (6B)
alza rise (8A)
amable friendly
amante *m., f.* lover
amar to love (7B)
amargo/a bitter (3B)
amarillo/a yellow (2B)
Amazonas: río Amazonas Amazon River
amazónico/a *adj.* Amazon
ambicioso/a ambitious (1B)
ambiente *m.* atmosphere; **medio ambiente** environment (6B)
ambigüedad *f.* ambiguity
ambos/as *pl.* both
amenaza threat
americano/a American; **fútbol** (*m.*) **americano** football (4A)
amerindio/a *adj.* indigenous to the Americas
amigo/a friend
amistad *f.* friendship (7B)
amor *m.* love
amoroso/a affectionate, loving
amortizar (c) una deuda to pay off a debt (8A); **amortizar una hipoteca** to pay off a mortgage (8A)
amplio/a ample, broad
amueblado/a furnished (4B)
amuleto amulet
analfabetismo illiteracy (8B)
análisis *m. inv.* analysis
analista *m., f.* analyst; **analista de sistemas** systems analyst (9B)
analítico/a analytical
anaranjado/a orange (*color*) (2B)
andar *irreg.* to walk; **andar en bicicleta** to ride a bicycle (4A); **rueda de andar** treadmill (4A)
andino/a Andean
anfitrión, anfitriona host, hostess
ángel *m.* angel
anglohablante *m., f.* English speaker; *adj.* English-speaking
angloparlante *m., f.* English speaker
animal *m.* animal
animar to encourage (9A); to animate; to energize
aniversario anniversary
anoche *adv.* last night
anotar to note, take note of
ansioso/a worried, anxious (5B)
Antártida Antarctica (6B)
ante *prep.* before; faced with; in the presence of
antemano: de antemano ahead of time
anteojos *pl.* glasses (*vision*)
antepasado/a ancestor

antes *adv.* before; **antes de** (*prep.*) + *inf.* before (*doing something*); **antes (de) que** *conj.* before (7B)
anticipación *f.*: **con dos horas de anticipación** two hours ahead of time
anticipar to anticipate, foresee
antiguo/a old
antioxidante antioxidizing
antirrobo/a antitheft; **seguro antirrobo** antitheft insurance (8A)
antropología anthropology (P)
antropólogo/a anthropologist
anuncio advertisement; announcement; **anuncio publicitario** commercial (8B)
añadir to add
año year (1B); **cada año** each year; **¿cuántos años cumples?** how many years old are you (*turning*) (*fam. s.*)? (4A); **cumplir... años** to be . . . old (*on a birthday*) (4A); **hace... años . . .** years ago; **tener** (*irreg.*)**... años** to be . . . years old (2A)
apagar (gu) to turn off (*light*) (5A)
aparato appliance; **aparato doméstico** household appliance (4B); **aparato electrónico** electronic device (5A)
aparecer (zc) to appear
aparente apparent
apariencia appearance
apartamento apartment (4B)
aparte *adv.* apart; besides; **hoja de papel aparte** separate piece of paper
apasionado/a passionate (1B)
apatía apathy
apático/a apathetic
apellido last name; **¿cuál es su apellido?** what's his/her last name? (P); **¿cuál es tu apellido?** what's your (*fam. s.*) last name? (P); **mi apellido es...** my last is . . . (P)
apenas *adv.* hardly; barely
aperitivo appetizer
apetecer (zc) to appeal, be pleasing (5A)
aplicarse (qu) to apply oneself
apodarse to be nicknamed
apoyar to support (8B)
apoyo support
apreciar to appreciate (9A)
aprender to learn (1B)
apresurar to rush
aprobar (ue) to approve, pass (8B)
apropiado/a appropriate (8B)
aprovecharse (de) to take advantage (of) (9A)
aproximadamente approximately
apuntar to note, jot down
apunte *m.* note; **tomar apuntes** to take notes (1A)
apurado/a hurried, rushed
aquel, aquella *adj.* that (over there) (2B); *pron.* that one (over there) (2B)

aquello *neut. pron.* that (2B); that thing (2B)
aquí here (2B)
árabe *n., adj. m., f.* Arab
araña spider (9A)
árbol *m.* tree; **árbol genealógico** family tree; **subirse a los árboles** to climb trees (5A)
archipiélago archipelago, group of islands
archivo archive, file (5A)
área *f.* (*but* **el área**) area
arena sand
argentino/a *n., adj.* Argentine
arma *f.* (*but* **el arma**) **de fuego** firearm
armado/a armed; **fuerzas armadas** armed forces
armario closet (4B)
armonía harmony, agreement
arquitecto/a architect (9B)
arquitectura architecture (9B); **arquitectura paisajista** landscape architecture
arreglar to fix
arrepentirse (ie, i) (de) to be sorry (about); to regret (7B)
arriba *prep.* up
arriesgado/a daring, risk-taking
arrogante arrogant (1B)
arroz *m.* rice (3B)
arruinar to ruin
arte *m.* (*but* **las artes**) art (9B); *pl.* arts (P)
arterial: presión (*f.*) **arterial** blood pressure (7A)
artículo article (8B)
artista *m., f.* artist
artístico/a artistic
ascendencia heritage
ascensor *m.* elevator
asegurado/a insured
asesinar to murder
asesor(a) consultant (9B)
así thus, so; **así así** so-so, fair; **así que** so (that), therefore
Asia Asia (6B)
asiático/a *n., adj.* Asian
asiáticoamericano *n., adj.* Asian-American
asiento chair (6A)
asignar to assign
asistente (*m., f.*) **de vuelo** flight attendant (6A)
asistir (a) to attend (1B)
asociación *f.* association
asociado/a associated; **Estado Libre Asociado** Free Associated State, Commonwealth
asociar to associate; to combine
aspecto aspect; appearance
aspiración *f.* aspiration, hope (9B)

aspiradora vacuum (4B); **pasar la aspiradora** to vacuum (4B)
aspirina aspirin (7A)
astronomía astronomy (P)
astrónomo/a astronomer (9B)
astuto/a astute, clever (1B)
asumir to assume
asunto subject, topic, issue
atacar (qu) to attack
atajo shortcut
atención f. attention
atender (ie) to wait on (6A)
atentado n. attack
atento/a attentive (7B)
atlántico/a: océano Atlántico Atlantic Ocean
atleta m., f. athlete (4A)
atlético/a athletic
atracción f. attraction; pl. amusements
atractivo/a attractive
atrapado/a trapped
atrasado/a backward
atravesar (ie) to cross; to run through (river)
atrevido/a daring (8B)
atribuirse (y) todo el mérito to take all the credit (9A)
atún m. tuna (3B)
audiencia audience
auditorio/a auditorium (P)
aumentar to augment, increase
aumento n. increase
aun adv. even
aún adv. still, yet
aunque although
ausencia absence
Australia Australia (6B)
auto car
autobús m. bus (6A); **parada de autobuses** bus stop (2A)
autoconsciente m., f. self-conscious
automático/a automatic; **cajero automático** ATM (2A); **contestador** (m.) **automático** answering machine (5A)
automóvil m. automobile (8A); **seguro de automóvil** automobile insurance (8A)
autonomía individual political entity or region (Sp.)
autónomo/a autonomous
autoridad f. authority
autorizar (c) to authorize
autostop m.: **hacer** (irreg.) **autostop** to hitchhike
avance m. advance
avanzar (c) to advance
ave f. (but **el ave**) bird; pl. poultry (3B)
aventurarse to risk
aventurero/a adventurous
avergonzado/a embarrassed (7A)
averiguar (averigüo) to find out

avión m. airplane (6A)
ayer yesterday (4A)
ayuda n. help; **pedir (i, i) ayuda** to ask for help
ayudante m., f. helper; assistant (9B)
ayudar to help (8B)
ayuntamiento city (town) hall
azteca n. m., f.; adj. Aztec
azúcar m. sugar (8A); **cañaveral** (m.) **de azúcar** sugar cane field
azul blue (2B)

B

bailar to dance (1A); **salir** (irreg.) **a bailar** to go dancing
baile m. dance
baja n. fall (stocks) (8A)
bajar to go down (8A); **bajar de** to get off (6A); **bajar de peso** to lose weight
bajo prep. under
bajo/a adj. short (height); low (3A); **los Países Bajos** The Netherlands
balcón m. balcony (4B)
bambalina: tras bambalinas behind the scenes
banana banana (3B)
bancario/a adj. banking, financial
banco bank (2A)
banda band
bandeja tray
bandera flag
bañar to bathe (9A); **bañarse** to take a bath (5A)
bañera bathtub (4B)
baño bathroom (4B); **con baño (privado)** with a (private) bathroom (6A); **traje** (m.) **de baño** bathing suit (2B)
bar m. bar (2A)
barato/a inexpensive, cheap (2B)
barbacoa n. barbecue
barco ship, boat; **navegar (gu) en barco** to sail (4A)
barra bar; **barra de frutas** fruit bar (3B); **barra de granola** granola bar (3B)
barrer (el piso) to sweep (the floor) (4B)
barrio neighborhood (2A)
basar to base, support
base f. base, foundation; **a base de** based on
básico/a basic
basquetbol m. basketball (4A); **jugar (ue) (gu) al basquetbol** to play basketball
bastante adv. somewhat, rather (1B)
basura garbage; **sacar (qu) la basura** to take out the trash (4B)
basurero landfill (6B)
bata robe (2B)
bebé m., f. baby
beber to drink (1B)

bebida n. drink; **bebida alcohólica** alcoholic drink
béisbol m. baseball (4A)
beisbolista m., f. baseball player
belleza beauty
bello/a beautiful
beneficios pl. benefits
berenjena eggplant
besar to kiss (7B)
beso n. kiss
biblioteca library (P)
bibliotecario/a librarian (9B)
bicicleta bicycle; **andar** (irreg.) **en bicicleta** to ride a bicycle (4A)
bien adv. well; **caerle** (irreg.) **bien a alguien** to like someone (5A); **combinar bien** to go well with (clothing) (2B); **llevarse bien con** to get along well with (5A); **manejar bien** to manage well (8A); **¿me queda bien?** does it fit me? (2B); **pasarlo bien** to have a good time (4A); **portarse bien** to behave well (5A); **quedarle bien** to fit well
bienes m. pl.: **bienes fabricados** manufactured goods (8A); **bienes raíces** real estate (8A)
bienestar m. well-being
bilingüe bilingual
bilingüismo bilingualism
billar m. s. pool, billiards
billete m. ticket (Sp.)
biodegradable: producto biodegradable biodegradable product (6B)
biografía biography
biología biology (P)
biólogo/a biologist (9B)
bistec m. steak (3B)
blanco/a white (2B); **vino blanco** white wine (3B)
blando/a soft (3B)
blindar to shield
blusa blouse (2B)
boca mouth (7A)
bocacalle f. intersection
boda wedding (5B); **padrino de boda** groomsman
bodega wine cellar
bolero love song
boleto ticket (6A)
bolígrafo pen
boliviano/a n., adj. Bolivian
bolsa purse (2B); **Bolsa de valores** stock market (8A)
bolso pocketbook; handbag
bonito/a pretty
bono voucher
borrador m. eraser (P)
bosque m. (lluvioso) (rain)forest (6B)
botana (Mex.) appetizer
botas pl. boots (2B)

botella bottle; **botella de plástico** plastic bottle (6B); **botella de vidrio** glass bottle (6B)

botón *m.* button

botones *m. inv.* bellhop (6A)

Brasil *m.* Brazil

brasileño/a Brazilian

bravo/a wild

brazo arm (7A)

brécol *m.* broccoli

bretaña: Gran Bretaña Great Britain

breve *adj.* brief

brillar to shine

brindar to toast

brindis *m.* toast (4A)

británico/a *adj.* British

bróculi *m.* broccoli (3B)

bruto/a: producto nacional bruto gross national product

bucear to snorkel (6B)

buen, bueno/a good (1B); **buen provecho** enjoy your meal; **buenas noches** good night (P); **buenas tardes** good afternoon/evening (P); **buenos días** good morning (P); **es buena idea** it's a good idea (2B); **estar** (*irreg.*) **a buen precio** it's a good price; **estar** (*irreg.*) **en buena forma** to be in good shape (4A); **hace buen tiempo** it's good weather (1B)

bufanda scarf (2B)

burlador(a) *adj.* seducer

burlarse de otros to make fun of others

buscar (qu) to look for (1A); **estoy buscando…** I'm looking for . . . (2B)

búsqueda *n.* search; **hacer** (*irreg.*) **una búsqueda** to do a search (5A)

C

caballero gentleman

caballo horse; **montar a caballo** to go horseback riding (6B)

cabello hair

cabeza head (7A); **dolor** (*m.*) **de cabeza** headache

cabezón(a) headstrong (5A)

cacahuete *m.* peanut; **mantequilla de cacahuete** peanut butter (3B)

cacao cocoa (8A)

cacique *m.* chief (*of a tribe*)

cada *inv.* each (1A); **cada año** each year; **cada día** every day; **cada mes** each month; **cada uno** each one; **cada vez** each time; **cada vez más** more and more

cadena (TV) network (8B)

caer(se) *irreg.* to fall; **caerle bien/mal a alguien** to (dis)like someone (5A); **¿en qué día (mes) cae… ?** what day (month) is . . . ?

café *m.* **(descafeinado)** (decaffeinated) coffee (3B); **café con leche** coffee with milk; **charlar en un café** to chat in a cafe (6B); **tomar café** to drink coffee (1A)

cafetera coffeepot (4B)

cafetería cafeteria (P)

caída *n.* drop

caja box; cashier's station, checkout counter (2B); **caja de cartón** cardboard box (6B)

cajero/a teller (8A); **cajero automático** ATM (2A)

cajón *m.* large box

calcetines *m. pl.* socks (2B)

calculadora calculator (5A)

calcular to calculate

cálculo calculus

calendario calendar

calidad *f.* quality

caliente hot; **chocolate** (*m.*) **caliente** hot chocolate (3B); **té** (*m.*) **caliente** hot tea (3B)

callar to silence someone; *refl.* to shut up

calle *f.* street (6A)

calmado/a calm

calmante *m.* tranquilizer

calor *m.* heat; **hace (mucho) calor** it's (very) hot (1B)

caloría calorie; **quemar calorías** to burn calories (4A)

calvo/a bald (3A)

calzar (c): ¿qué número calza? what size shoe do you (*form. s.*) wear? (2B)

cama bed (4B); **cama matrimonial** queen bed (4B); **cama sencilla** twin bed (4B); **hacer** (*irreg.*) **la cama** to make the bed (4B)

cámara digital digital camera (5A)

camarero/a waiter, waitress

camarones *m. pl.* shrimp (3B)

cambiar (por) to change, exchange (for); **cambiar de canal** to change channels (5A)

cambio change; **en cambio** on the other hand

caminar to walk (4A)

camino road; **camino a** on the way to

camión *m.* truck; bus (*Mex.*)

camisa shirt (2B)

camiseta T-shirt (2B)

campanario bell tower

campaña campaign

campeonato championship (4A)

campesino/a peasant

camping: hacer (*irreg.*) **camping** to go camping (6B)

campo country(side); field (*of work*) (9B); **¿cuál es tu campo?** what's your major? (P)

canadiense *n., adj.* Canadian

canal *m.* canal; **cambiar de canal** to change channels (5A); **canal de televisión** television channel

canario canary (9A)

cancelar to cancel

cancha (de tenis) (tennis) court (4A)

canción *f.* song

candidato/a candidate

canoa canoe; **remar en canoa** to go canoeing (6B)

canoso/a: pelo canoso gray hair (3A)

cansado/a tired (7A)

cansarse to tire (7A)

cantante *m., f.* singer

cantar to sing (1A)

cantidad *f.* quantity

cañaveral (*m.*) **de azúcar** sugar cane field

caótico/a chaotic (1B)

capa de ozono ozone layer (6B)

capilla chapel (2A)

cápita: renta per cápita per capita income

capital *f.* capital (*city*)

capitán *m.* captain

captar to grasp

cara *n.* face (7A)

característica characteristic

caracterizar (c) to characterize

carbohidrato carbohydrate (3B)

cardíaco/a: infarto cardíaco heart attack

cardiopatía cardiopathy

cargar (gu) to charge

cargo: hacerse (*irreg.*) **cargo de** to take charge of (*something*)

Caribe *m.* Caribbean (Sea)

caribeño/a *n., adj.* of or from the Caribbean

caries *f. inv.* cavity

cariño affection; **tenerle** (*irreg.*) **cariño a alguien** to be fond of someone (7B)

cariñoso/a affectionate (7B)

carnaval *m.* carnival; **Martes** (*m.*) **de Carnaval** Mardi Gras (4A)

carne *f.* meat (3B); **carne de res** beef (3B)

carnero *n.* ram

carnicería butcher's shop

caro/a expensive (2B)

carrera major; career; **¿qué carrera haces?** what's your (*fam. s.*) major? (P)

carretera highway

carro *m.* car

carta letter

cartel *m.* poster (4B)

cartelera billboard

cartera wallet (2B)

cartón *m.* cardboard; **caja de cartón** cardboard box (6B)

casa house (4B); **casa particular** private residence (4B); **casa privada** private residence (4B); **compañero/a de casa**

housemate (4B); **limpiar la casa (entera)** to clean the (whole) house (4B); **regresar a casa** to go home (1A)

casado/a married (3A)

casamentero/a matchmaker

casarse (con) to marry, get married (5B)

casi almost; **casi nunca** almost never; **casi siempre** almost always

caso case; **en caso de que** *conj.* in case (7B)

castaño/a brown (3A)

castellano *n.* Spanish (*language*)

castellano/a *adj.* Castilian

castigar (gu) to punish (7B)

castillo castle

casualidad *f.* chance; coincidence

catalán/catalana *n., adj.* Catalonian

catálogo *n.* catalog

cataratas *pl.* waterfall (6B)

catástrofe *f.* catastrophe

catedral *f.* cathedral (2A)

categoría category; class

catolicismo Catholicism

católico/a *n., adj.* Catholic

catorce fourteen (1A)

causa cause; **a causa de** because of

causar to cause

cautela caution

cazuela casserole

CD: reproductor (*m.*) **de CD** CD player (5A)

cebolla onion (3B)

celebración *f.* celebration

celebrar to celebrate (4A)

célebre famous

celos *pl.* jealousy (7B); **tener** (*irreg.*) **celos** to be jealous

celoso/a jealous; **estar** (*irreg.*) **celoso/a** to be jealous (7A)

celular: (teléfono) celular cell phone (5A)

cena dinner (3B)

cenar to eat/have (for) dinner (3B); **cenar en un restaurante elegante** to eat in a fancy restaurant (6B)

cenizas *pl.* ashes

censurar to judge

centígrado/a centigrade

centro downtown (2A); **centro comercial** shopping center, mall (2A); **centro estudiantil** student center/union (2A)

Centroamérica Central America

centroamericano/a *n., adj. of or from Central America*

cepas *pl.* vine stocks

cepillo brush

cerca de *prep.* close to (2A)

cerdo pork (9A); **chuleta de cerdo** pork chop (3B)

cereal (cocido) (cooked) cereal (3B)

cerebral cerebral (1B)

cerebro brain (8A)

ceremonia ceremony

cero zero (1A)

cerrar (ie) to close (2A)

cerveza beer; **tomar cerveza** to drink beer (1A)

chamán *m.* shaman

champiñones *m. pl.* mushrooms (3B)

champú *m.* shampoo

chapulín *m.* grasshopper

chaqueta jacket (2B)

charadas: juego de charadas charades

charlar to chat (1A); **charlar en un café** to chat in a cafe (6B)

chatarro/a: comida chatarra junk food

chau ciao

cheque *m.* check (8A); **cheque de viajero** traveler's check (8A)

chequear to check

chícharo pea (3B)

chico/a *n. m., f.* boy, girl (P); *adj.* small

chileno/a *n., adj.* Chilean

chimpancé *m.* chimpanzee

chisme *m.* gossip; **contar (ue) chismes** to gossip (9A)

chismear to gossip

chismoso/a gossipy (1B)

chiste *m.* joke

chocante shocking (8B)

chocar (qu) to run into

chocolate *m.* chocolate; **chocolate caliente** hot chocolate (3B)

chubasco rainstorm

chuleta de cerdo pork chop (3B)

cibercafé *m.* cybercafe

ciclismo cycling; **hacer** (*irreg.*) **ciclismo estacionario** to ride a stationary bike (4A)

cielo sky; heaven

cien, ciento one hundred (2A); **ciento uno/a** (2B); **por ciento** percent

cien mil one hundered thousand (5B)

ciencia science; **ciencias naturales** natural sciences (P); **ciencias políticas** political science (P); **ciencias sociales** social sciences (P)

científico/a scientist (9B); *adj.* scientific

cierto/a certain; true

cifra number, figure

cigarrillo cigarette

cima top

cinco five (1A)

cincuenta fifty (2A)

cine *m.* movie theater (2A); the movies; **ir** (*irreg.*) **al cine** to go to the movies

cinta cassette

cintura waist

cinturón *m.* belt (2B); **abrocharse el cinturón** to fasten one's seatbelt

circulación *f.* circulation; traffic

círculo circle

circunstancia circumstance

cirugía surgery

cirujano/a surgeon

cita appointment; date (5A)

ciudad *f.* city (2A)

ciudadano/a citizen (8B)

cívico/a civic; **responsabilidad** (*f.*) **cívica** civic duty (8B); **reunión** (*f.*) **cívica** town meeting (8B)

civil: ingeniería civil civil engineering (P); **ingeniero/a civil** civil engineer (9B)

civilización *f.* civilization

clarificación *f.* clarification

claro/a clear; light

clase *f.* class (P); **clase media** middle class; **clase turística** tourist class (6A); **compañero/a de clase** classmate; **primera clase** first class (6A); **¿qué clases tienes este semestre/trimestre?** what classes do you (*fam. s.*) have this semester/quarter? (P); **sala de clase** classroom (P); **tengo una clase de...** I have a(n) . . . class (P); **tomar una clase** to take a class (1A)

clasificación *f.* classification

clasificar (qu) to classify

clave *f.* key

clic: hacer (*irreg.*) **clic** to click (5A)

cliente *m., f.* customer (2B)

clima *m.* climate

clínica clinic

coágulo clot

cobrar to charge (*a fee*) (8A)

cocido/a cooked (3B); **cereal** (*m.*) **cocido** cooked cereal (3B)

coche *m.* car

cocina kitchen; cooking (4B)

cocinar to cook (4A)

cocinero/a cook (6A)

codiciado/a coveted

código code

codo elbow (7A)

coexistir to coexist

cognado cognate

coincidencia coincidence

coincidir to coincide

cola tail (*of an animal*); line (*of people*); **hacer** (*irreg.*) **cola** to wait (stand) in line (6A)

colaborar to collaborate (9A)

colección *f.* collection

coleccionar to collect; **coleccionar estampillas** to collect stamps (4A); **coleccionar monedas** to collect coins (4A)

colega *m., f.* colleague (9A)

colegio high school

colesterol *m.* cholesterol

colgar (ue) (gu) to hang

coliflor *f.* cauliflower (3B)

colina hill (6B)

colocar (qu) to place

colombiano/a *n., adj.* Colombian
colonia colony
colonizar (c) to colonize (5B)
color *m.* color
colorear to color (5A)
columna column
comandante commander
combatir to fight
combinación *f.* combination
combinar to combine; **combinar bien** to go well with (*clothing*) (2B)
combustibles (*m.*) **fósiles** fossil fuels (6B)
comedia comedy (8B)
comedor *m.* dining room (4B)
comentar to comment, make comments on; to discuss
comentario comment; remark; *pl.* commentaries
comenzar (ie) (c) to begin
comer to eat (1B); **dar** (*irreg.*) **de comer** to feed (9A)
comercial: centro comercial shopping center, mall (2A)
comercio business (P); **Tratado de Libre Comercio (TLC)** North American Free Trade Agreement (NAFTA)
comestible *m.* food item (8A)
cometer to commit
cómico/a funny, comical (1B); **tiras cómicas** comics (5A)
comida food; meal; **comida chatarra** junk food; **comida rápida** fast food (3B)
comienzo *n.* beginning
comisión *f.* commission (8A)
como as, like; **tan pronto como** as soon as (9B)
¿cómo? how (1B); **¿cómo es?** what is he/she/it like? what are you (*form. s.*) like? (3A); **¿cómo se llama (él/ella)?** what's his/her name? (P); **¿cómo se llega a… ?** how do you get to . . . ? (6A); **¿cómo te llamas?** what's your (*fam. s.*) name? (P)
cómoda dresser, chest of drawers (4B)
comodidades *f. pl.* amenities, conveniences
cómodo/a comfortable
compañero/a companion; **compañero/a de casa** housemate (4B); **compañero/a de clase** classmate; **compañero/a de cuarto** roommate (4B)
compañía company; **servir (i, i) de compañía** to give, keep company (9A)
comparación *f.* comparison
comparar to compare
compartir to share
compasión *f.* compassion
competición *f.* competition
competidor(a) competitive (9A)
competir (i, i) to compete (4A)
complemento *gram.* pronoun

completar to complete
completo/a complete; **pensión** (*f.*) **completa** room and all meals (6A)
comportamiento behavior (9A)
comportarse to behave, act
composición *f.* composition
comprar to buy (2B); **comprar recuerdos** to buy souvenirs (6B)
compras purchases; **de compras** shopping (2B)
comprender to understand (1B); to encompass
comprensivo/a understanding (7B)
comprometer to compromise; to involve; **comprometerse (con)** to get engaged (to) (7B)
compuesto/a *adj.* compound
compulsivo/a compulsive
computación *f.* computer science (9B)
computadora computer (P); **computadora portátil** laptop computer (5A)
común *adj.* common
comunicación *f.* communication; **medios** (*pl.*) **de communication** media (8B); *pl.* communications (P)
comunidad *f.* community
con with (P); **con baño privado** with a private bathroom (6A); **con frecuencia** frequently; **con tal (de) que** provided (that) (7B)
concentración *f.* concentration
concentrar to concentrate; to focus; **concentrarse en** to concentrate in, be concentrated in
concepto concept, idea
concierto concert; **ir** (*irreg.*) **a un concierto** to go to a concert (6B)
conclusión *f.* conclusion
concordancia *gram.* agreement
concurso contest; game show (8B)
condición *f.* condition
condicional *m. gram.* conditional
condimentos condiments
condominio condominium (4B)
conducir *irreg.* to drive; **sacar (qu) la licencia de conducir** to get a driver's license (5A)
conducta conduct, behavior
conductor(a) driver
conectar to connect (5A)
conejo rabbit (9A)
conexión *f.* connection
confesar (ie) to confess
confiable trustworthy (9A)
confiado/a trusting (1B)
confianza trust
confiar (confío) (en) to trust (in) (7B)
confidente confident
confirmar to confirm
conflicto conflict; **resolver (ue) conflictos** to resolve conflicts (9A)

confrontación *f.* confrontation
confrontar to confront
confundido/a confused (7A)
confundir to confuse; *refl.* to get confused (7A)
confusión *f.* confusion
confuso/a confusing
congelación *n. f.* freezing
congelado/a frozen
congelador *m.* freezer
congelar to freeze; **congelarse** to freeze up (*the screen*) (5A)
conjunto outfit; entirety
conmigo with me
conocer (zc) to know, be familiar with (*someone, something*) (3A)
conocido/a acquaintance (9A)
conocimiento awareness; *pl.* knowledge
conquista conquest (5B)
conquistar to conquer (5B); to succeed in seducing someone (7B)
consecuencia consequence
conseguir (i, i) (g) to get, obtain (4B); **conseguir** + *inf.* to succeed in (*doing something*) (4B)
consejo piece of advice; *pl.* advice
consenso consent
consentido *n.* whim, fancy
consentido/a indulged, spoiled
conservación *f.* conservation
conservador(a) conservative (1B)
conservar to preserve, conserve (6B)
consideración *f.* consideration
considerar to consider
consistir en to consist of
consolar (ue) to console (9A)
constante *adj.* constant
constitución *f.* constitution
constituir (y) to constitute
construir (y) to build (6B)
consultar to consult
consultorio doctor's office (7A)
consumidor(a) *n.* consumer
consumir to eat; to use up
consumo consumption
contabilidad *f.* accounting (P)
contacto contact
contador(a) accountant (9B)
contaminación *f.* pollution; **contaminación del agua** water pollution (6B); **contaminación del aire** air pollution (6B)
contaminar to contaminate (6B)
contar (ue) to count (2A); to tell (2A); **contar chismes** to gossip (9A)
contener (*like* **tener**) to contain
contenido *s.* contents
contento/a happy (7A)
contestador (*m.*) **automático** answering machine (5A)
contestar to answer

contexto context
contigo *fam. s.* with you
continente *m.* continent (6B)
continuación *f.* continuation; **a continuación** following
continuar (continúo) to continue
continuo/a continuous
contra: en contra opposed
contraer (*like* **traer**) to contract
contrario *n.* opposite, contrary
contraseña password (5A)
contraste *m.* contrast
contratar to hire
contrato lease (4B)
contribución *f.* contribution
contribuir (y) to contribute
controlar to control (8B); to inspect
controvertido/a controversial (8B)
convencer (z) to convince
conversación *f.* conversation
convertir (ie, i) to change; **convertirse en** to turn into
coordinación *f.* coordination
copa (wine) glass (6A)
copiar to copy (5A)
coqueto/a flirtatious (7B)
corazón *m.* heart (7A)
corbata necktie (2B)
cordillera mountain range (6B)
correcto/a correct
corregir (i, i) (j) to correct (9A)
correo mail (2A); post office; **correo electrónico** e-mail (5A)
correr to run (1B)
correspondencia correspondence
corresponder to correspond
correspondiente *adj.* corresponding
corriente *n. f.* current; *adj.* current, present; **agua** (*f.* [*but* **el agua**]) **corriente** running water; **cuenta corriente** checking account (8A); **estar** (*irreg.*) **al corriente** to be caught up (*with current events*) (8B)
corrupción *f.* corruption (8B)
cortar(se) to cut (oneself) (7A)
cortés courteous, polite (9A)
corto/a short (*except height*) (3A); **de corto plazo** short term (2B); **pantalones** (*m. pl.*) **cortos** shorts (2B)
cosa thing; **poner** (*irreg.*) **las cosas en orden** to put things in order (4B)
cosecha harvest
coser to sew
cosmético/a: cirugía cosmética cosmetic (plastic) surgery
cosmopolita *adj. m., f.* cosmopolitan
costa coast (6B)
costar (ue) to cost (2A)
costilla rib
costo cost, price

costumbre *f.* custom
cotidiano/a daily
creador(a) creative (1B)
crear to create
creativo/a creative
crecer (zc) to grow
creciente *adj.* growing
crédito credit (1A); **tarjeta de crédito** credit card (2B)
creencia belief
creer (y) (que) to believe (that) (1B); **creo que le queda un poco grande** I think it's a bit big on you (2B)
crema cream; **queso de crema** cream cheese (3B)
crianza upbringing
crimen *m.* crime; **crimen violento** violent crime (8B)
crisis *f.* crisis
cristiano/a *n., adj.* Christian
criticar (qu) to criticize (8B)
crítico/a critic
cronológico/a chronological
crucero cruise ship
crudo/a raw (3B)
cruel cruel (7B)
cruzar (c) to cross (6A)
cuaderno notebook
cuadra (city) block (6A)
cuadrado/a squared; **metros cuadrados** square meters (4B); **pies** (*m.*) **cuadrados** square feet (4B)
cuadro painting (4B); statistical chart; **de cuadros** plaid (2B)
cual: tal cual just as
¿cuál(es)? what? which? (1B); **¿cuál es su apellido?** what's his/her last name? (P); **¿cuál es su talla?** what size do you (*form. s.*) wear? (2B); **¿cuál es tu apellido** what's your (*fam. s.*) last name? (P); **¿cuál es tu campo?** what's your major? (P)
cualquier(a) any
cuando when(ever) (9B); **de vez en cuando** once in a while (3B)
¿cuándo? when? (1B)
cuanto: en cuanto as soon as (9B); **en cuanto a** with regard to; **en unos cuantos días** in a few days (1B)
cuánto *pron.* **¿a cuánto sale?** how much is it?; **¿cuánto hay de aquí a…** how far is it from here to . . . ? (6A)
¿cuántos/as? how many? (1B); **¿cuántos años cumples?** how many years old are you (*turning*) (*fam. s.*)? (4A); **¿cuántos años tiene… ?** how old is . . . ?; **¿cuántos años tienes?** how old are you (*fam. s.*)?
cuarenta forty (2A)
cuarto *n.* quarter (*of an hour*); fourth; room (4B); **compañero/a de cuarto** roommate

(4B); **menos cuarto** a quarter to (*hour*) (1A); **servicio de cuarto** room service (6A); **y cuarto** a quarter past (*hour*) (1A)
cuarto/a fourth (4A)
cuatro four (1A)
cuatrocientos/as four hundred (2B)
cuatrocientos/as mil four hundred thousand (5B)
cubano/a *n., adj.* Cuban
cubierto/a (*p.p. of* **cubrir**) covered
cubiertos *pl.* silverware (6A)
cubrir (*p.p.* **cubierto/a**) to cover
cuchara spoon (6A)
cuchillo knife (6A)
cuello neck (7A)
cuenta bill (6A); check; **cuenta corriente** checking account (8A); **cuenta de ahorros** savings account (8A); **darse** (*irreg.*) **cuenta de** to realize
cuento story
cuerda cord; **saltar la cuerda** to jump rope
cuerno horn; **ponerle** (*irreg.*) **los cuernos (a alguien)** to be unfaithful to (someone)
cuero leather (2B)
cuerpo body; **partes** (*f. pl.*) **del cuerpo** parts of the body (7A)
cuestión *f.* question
cuidado care
cuidar (de) to take care (of) (9A)
culpa fault; **echar(le) la culpa (a alguien)** to blame (someone) (9A)
culto devotion (*to a god or belief*)
cultura culture
cumpleaños *m. inv.* birthday (4A)
cumplido compliment
cumplir (con) to fulfill, carry out; **¿cuántos años cumples?** how many years old are you (*turning*) (*fam. s.*)? (4A); **cumplir… años** to be . . . old (*on a birthday*) (4A); **cumplir las promesas** to keep one's word (9A)
cuñado/a brother-in-law, sister-in-law; *pl.* siblings-in-law
curandero/a healer
curar to cure
cursi tacky (8B); cheesy
cursivo/a: letra (*s.*) **cursiva** italics
curso course
cuy *m.* guinea pig (9A)
cuyo/a/os/as whose

D

dama lady; **dama de honor** bridesmaid
dañar to hurt, harm (8B)
dañino/a harmful
daño damage, hurt
dar *irreg.* to give (3B); **dar de comer** to feed (9A); **dar la vuelta a** to go around

(*something*); **dar las gracias** to thank; **dar un paseo** to take a walk (4A); **dar una fiesta** to throw a party (4A); **darle escalofríos a alguien** to give someone chills (7B); **darle rabia (a alguien)** to make (someone) angry; **darse cuenta de** to realize; **darse la mano** to shake hands (7B)

dato piece of information; *pl.* data, facts

de *prep.* of (P); from (P); **de compras** shopping (2B); **de corto/largo plazo** short/long term (9B); **de cuadros** plaid (2B); **¿de dónde eres?** where are you (*fam. s.*) from? (P); **de estatura mediana** of medium height (3A): **de ida** one-way (6A); **de ida y vuelta** round-trip (6A); **de la mañana** in the morning (A.M.) (1A); **de la noche** in the evening (night) (P.M.) (1A); **de la tarde** in the afternoon (1A); **de las… hasta las…** from . . . (*hour*) to (*hour*) (1A); **de lunares** polka-dotted (2B); **¿de qué tamaño es… ?** what size is . . . ? (4B); **de rayas** striped (2B); **de repente** suddenly; **de venta** for sale (4B); **de vez en cuando** once in a while (3B); **es de…** it's made of . . . (2B); **soy de…** I'm from . . . (P)

debajo de under, below (2A)

deber *n. m.* duty (8B)

deber + *inf.* ought to, should (*do something*); to owe (8A)

debido a due to

débil weak

década decade (5B)

decidido/a decisive

decidir to decide

decir *irreg.* (*p.p.* **dicho/a**) to say (2A)

decisión *f.* decision

declaración *f.* statement

declarar to declare

dedicación *f.* dedication

dedicarse (qu) a to dedicate oneself to

dedo finger (7A); **dedo del pie** toe (7A)

deducción *f.* deduction

deducir (*like* **conducir**) to deduct; to infer

defecto defect

defender (ie) to defend (9A)

defensor(a) *n.* defender; *adj.* defensive

definición *f.* definition

definir to define

definitivo/a definitive

deforestación *f.* deforestation (6B)

degustar vinos to go wine tasting (6B)

dejar to leave; **dejar de** + *inf.* to stop (*doing something*); **dejar en paz** to leave alone; **dejar perplejo/a (a alguien)** to leave (someone) perplexed; **dejar (una) propina** to leave a tip (6A)

del (*contraction of* **de** + **el**) of/from the

delante de in front of (2A)

delgado/a thin (3A)

delicado/a delicate

delicioso/a delicious

demandar to demand

demás: los/las demás others (4A); **dirigir (j) a los demás** to lead others (9B)

demasiado *adv.* too, too much

demasiado/a *adj.* too much; *pl.* too many

democracia democracy

democrático/a democratic

demostrar (ue) to demonstrate; to show

demostrativo/a demonstrative

denotar to denote; to indicate

densidad *f.* density

denso/a heavy

dentista *m., f.* dentist

dentro (de) in, within, inside; **dentro de poco** in a little while (1B); **por dentro** within, (on the) inside

depender de to depend on

dependiente/a salesperson (2B)

deporte *m.* sport; **practicar (qu) un deporte** to practice a sport (1A)

deportivo/a *adj.* sport; **programa** (*m.*) **deportivo** sports show (8B)

depositar to deposit

depresión *f.* **(económica)** (economic) depression (5B)

deprimido/a depressed (5B)

deprimir(se) to depress, become depressed (7A)

derecha *n.* right-hand side; **a la derecha (de)** to the right (of) (2A); **doblar a la derecha** to turn right

derecho *n.* right (*legal*) (8B); law (9B); **derechos humanos** human rights (8B); **seguir (i, i) (g) derecho** to continue straight ahead (6A)

derramar to spill

derrocar (qu) to defeat

derrochador(a) wasteful (8A)

derrotar to defeat

desafío *n.* challenge

desafortunadamente unfortunately

desagradable unpleasant

desahogarse (gu) con to take it out on

desarrollado/a developed; **país** (*m.*) **desarrollado** developed country (8A)

desarrollar to develop

desarrollo (sustenable) (sustainable) development; **país** (*m.*) **en vías de desarrollo** developing country (8A)

desastre *m.* **(natural)** (natural) disaster (5B)

desastroso/a desastrous

desaventajado/a disadvantaged

desayunar to eat/have (for) breakfast (3B)

desayuno breakfast (3B)

descafeinado/a decaffeinated (3B); **café** (*m.*) **descafeinado** decaffeinated coffee

descansar to rest (1A)

descapotable convertible

descargar (gu) to download (5A)

descendiente *m., f.* descendant

descomponer (*like* **poner**) decompose (6B)

desconectar to unplug, disconnect

desconfiado/a untrusting (1B)

desconocido/a unknown

describir (*p.p.* **descrito/a**) to describe (1B)

descripción *f.* description

descubierto/a (*p.p. of* **descubrir**) discovered

descubrimiento discovery (5B)

descuento discount

descuidar to neglect

desde *prep.* from; **desde la(s)… hasta la(s)…** from . . . until . . . (*time*)

desear to want, desire (1A)

desechable disposable; **producto desechable** disposable product (6B)

desechos *pl.* wastes

desempleo unemployment; **tasa de desempleo** unemployment rate (8A)

deseo *n.* wish, desire (9B)

desierto desert (6B)

desilusionado/a disillusioned

desleal disloyal (1B)

desobedecer (zc) to disobey (3A)

despacio/a slow

despedirse (i, i) to say good-bye

despegar (gu) to take off (*plane*)

despejado/a clear; **está despejado** it's clear (*weather*) (1B)

desperdiciar to waste (6B)

desperdicios *pl.* waste (6B)

despertador *m.* alarm clock

despertarse (ie) to wake up (2A)

despreciar to despise (7B)

después *adv.* after; **después de** *prep.* after; **después (de) que** *conj.* after (9B)

destacado/a outstanding

destacar (qu) to stand out

destino destination; destiny, fate

destrucción *f.* destruction

detalle *m.* detail

detallista *adj. m., f.* detail-oriented (7B)

detergente *m.* detergent (4B)

determinar to determine

detestar to detest (7B)

detrás de *adv.* behind (2A)

deuda debt (8A); **amortizar (c) una deuda** to pay off a debt (8A)

devoción *f.* devotion

devolver (ue) (*p.p.* **devuelto/a**) to return (*something*)

devoto/a devout

devuelto/a (*p.p. of* **devolver**) returned

día *m.* day (1A); **buenos días** good morning (P); **cada día** every day; **Día de Acción de Gracias** Thanksgiving (4A); **Día de la Madre (del Padre)** Mother's (Father's) Day; **Día de los Enamorados** St. Valentine's Day (4A); **Día de los Reyes Magos** Epiphany (January 6), Day of the Magi; **Día de San Patricio** St. Patrick's Day (4A); **Día de San Valentín** St. Valentine's Day (4A); **día del santo** saint's day; **Día del Trabajo** Labor Day; **día festivo** holiday (4A); **¿en qué día cae... ?** what day is . . . ?; **hoy en día** nowadays; **¿qué día es hoy?** what day is it today? (1A); **todos los días** every day (1A)

diabetes *f.* diabetes

dialecto dialect

diálogo dialogue

diario *m.* newspaper

diario/a *adj.* daily

dibujar to draw (4A)

dibujo drawing

diccionario dictionary

dicho/a (*p.p. of* **decir**) said

diciembre *m.* December (1B)

dictador(a) dictator

dictadura dictatorship

diecinueve nineteen (1A)

dieciocho eighteen (1A)

dieciséis sixteen (1A)

diecisiete seventeen (1A)

diente *m.* tooth; **lavarse los dientes** to brush one's teeth (5A)

dieta *n.* diet

dietético/a: refresco dietético diet soft drink (3B)

diez ten (1A)

diez mil ten thousand (5B)

diferencia difference; **a diferencia de** unlike

diferenciar (de) to be different (from)

diferente (de) different (from/than)

difícil difficult (5B)

dificultad *f.* difficulty

difundirse to diffuse, spread

digestivo/a digestive

digital: cámara digital digital camera (5A)

Dinamarca Denmark

dinamismo dynamism, quality of being dynamic

dinero money (2B); **sacar (qu) dinero** to withdraw money (8A)

dinosaurio dinosaur

dios(a) god, goddess

diplomático/a diplomat

dirección *f.* direction; address (4B)

directo/a direct; straight; **pensar (ie) de manera directa** to think in a direct (linear) manner (9B); **vuelo directo** direct flight (6A)

director(a) director (9B)

dirigir (j) to direct; **dirigir a los demás** to lead others (9B); **dirigirse a** to direct oneself toward

disco: disco compacto compact disc; **disco duro** hard drive (5A)

discoteca discotheque (2A)

discreto/a discreet (1B)

discriminación *f.* discrimination (8B)

disculpar to excuse

disculpas: pedir (*irreg.*) **disculpas** to apologize

discusión *f.* discussion

discutir to discuss; to argue (7B)

diseñador(a) designer; **diseñador(a) de sitios** Web site designer (9B)

diseñar to draw; to design

disfrutar to enjoy

disponible available

disposición *f.* disposition

dispositivo device

dispuesto/a ready, willing (9A)

disquete *m.* diskette (5A)

distancia distance; **mando a distancia** remote control (5A)

distante distant; far away

distinción *f.* distinction

distinguir (g) to distinguish

distinto/a different, distinct

distorsionado/a distorted (8B)

distorsionar to distort

distraer (*like* **traer**) to distract (8B)

distribución *f.* distribution

distrito (federal) (federal) district

diversidad *f.* diversity

diversión *f.:* **ir** (*irreg.*) **a un parque de diversiones** to go to an amusement park (6B)

diverso/a diverse

divertido/a fun (1B)

divertir (ie, i) to entertain (4A); **divertirse** to enjoy oneself (5B)

dividirse to divide

divinidad *f.* divinity, god-like being

divorciado/a divorced (3A)

divorciarse to divorce, get divorced (5B)

divorcio divorce (5B)

doblar to turn (6A); **doblar a la derecha/izquierda** to turn right/left

doble double

doce twelve (1A)

doctor(a) doctor

doctorado doctoral degree (9B)

documental *m.* documentary (8B)

documento document; **guardar documentos** to save documents (5A)

dólar *m.* dollar

doler (ue) to hurt, ache (7A)

dolor *m.* pain; **dolor de cabeza** headache

doméstico/a domestic; **aparato doméstico** household appliance (4B); **quehaceres** (*m.*) **domésticos** household chores (4B); **violencia doméstica** domestic violence (8B)

dominación *f.* domination

dominante dominant

dominar to dominate

domingo Sunday (1A)

dominicano/a *n., adj.* of or from the Dominican Republic

dominio *n.* control

don *m.* gift, skill; *title of respect used with a man's first name;* **tener** (*irreg.*) **don de gentes** to have a way with people (9B)

¿dónde? where? (1B); **¿de dónde eres?** where are you? (*fam. s.*) from? (P);

doña *title of respect used with a woman's first name*

dormir (ue, u) to sleep (2A); **dormirse** to fall asleep (5A)

dormitorio bedroom

dos two (1A)

dos mil two thousand (5B)

dos millones two million (5B)

doscientos/as two hundred (2B)

doscientos mil two hundred thousand (5B)

drama *m.* drama (8B)

drástico/a drastic

droga drug

drogadicción *f.* drug addiction (8B)

ducha shower (4B)

ducharse to shower, take a shower (5A)

duda doubt; **sin duda** without a doubt

dudar to doubt (8B)

dudoso/a doubtful

dueño/a owner (4B)

dulce *adj.* sweet (3B); *n. pl.* candy (3B); **pan** (*m.*) **dulce** sweet bread (*Mex.*) (3B)

duración *f.* duration

durante during

durar to last

durmiente: la Bella Durmiente Sleeping Beauty

duro/a hard; firm; **disco duro** hard drive (5A)

DVD: reproductor (*m.*) **de DVD** DVD player (5A); **sacar (qu) un DVD** to rent a DVD (4A)

E

e and (*used instead of* **y** *before words beginning with* **i** *or* **hi**)

echar to throw out (6B); **echar (le) la culpa (a alguien)** to blame (someone) (9A); **echar un vistazo** to look over; **echar una siesta** to take a nap

ecología ecology

ecológico/a ecological

economía economy (8A); *s.* economics (P)

económico/a economic; **depresión** (*f.*) **económica** economic depression (5B); **nivel económico** economic level

ecoturismo ecotourism

ecoturista *m., f.* ecotourist

ecoturístico/a *adj.* ecotourist

ecuatoriano/a *n., adj.* Ecuadorean

edad *f.* age (2A); **edad adulta** adulthood

edición *f.* edition

edificio building (P)

educación *f.* education

educar (qu) to educate (8B)

educativo/a educational

efectivo: en efectivo cash (money) (2B)

efecto effect; **efecto invernadero** greenhouse effect (6B)

eficaz (*pl.* **eficaces**) effective

egoísta *adj. m., f.* selfish, egotistical (1B)

ejecutivo/a executive

ejemplificar (qu) to exemplify

ejemplo example; **por ejemplo** for example

ejercer (z) to engage in

ejercicio exercise; **hacer** (*irreg.*) **ejercicio** to exercise (4A); **hacer** (*irreg.*) **ejercicio aeróbico** to do aerobics (4A)

ejército army

el *def. art. m.* the (P); **el/la mayor** the oldest (3A); **el/la menor** the youngest (3A)

él *sub. pron.* he (P); *obj. of prep.* him

elección *f.* election (3B)

electricidad *f.* electricity

eléctrico/a electric; **ingeniería eléctrica** electrical engineering (P); **ingeniero/a eléctrico/a** electrical engineer (9B)

electrónico/a electronic (8A); **agenda electrónica** electronic organizer, PDA (personal digital assistant) (5A); **aparato electrónico** electronic device (5A); **correo electrónico** e-mail (5A)

elegante elegant; **cenar en un restaurante elegante** to eat in a fancy restaurant (6B)

elegir (i, i) (j) to choose; to elect

elemento element

elevar to elevate, raise

eliminar to eliminate (8B)

ella *sub. pron.* she (P); *obj of prep.* her

ellos/as *sub. pron.* they (P); *obj. of prep.* them

embargo: sin embargo *conj.* however

emborracharse to get drunk

emergencia emergency

emocionado/a moved

emocional emotional (7B)

emocionante exciting (5B)

empanada turnover pie or pastry

emparejar to match

emperador(a) emperor, empress

empezar (ie) (c) to begin (2A); **empezar a** + *inf.* to begin to (*do something*)

empleado/a employee (9A)

emplear to use

empleo job; **anuncio de empleo** job ad

empresa company; **administración** (*f.*) **de empresas** business administration (P)

empresarial of or related to business

en in (2A); **en cambio** on the other hand; **en caso de que** in case (7B); **en cuanto** as soon as (9B); **en cuanto a** with regard to; **en punto** on the dot (*time*) (1A); **¿en qué día/mes cae… ?** what day/month is . . . ?; **¿en qué puedo servirle?** how may I help you? (2B); **en unos cuantos días** in a few days (1B)

enamorado/a (de) in love (with) (7A); **Día** (*m.*) **de los Enamorados** St. Valentine's Day (4A)

enamorarse (de) to fall in love (with) (5A)

encantado/a nice to meet you

encantador(a) delightful, charming (7B)

encantar to love (5A); **encantarle** to charm, delight (*someone*); to love (*thing*)

encargarse (de) to take charge (of)

encender (ie) to turn on (5A)

enchufe *m.* connection

encima de on top of (2A)

enclave *m.* enclave

encontrar (ue) to find (2B); **encontrarse con** to get together (meet) with

encuentro *n.* get-together; (chance) meeting (5B)

encuesta survey

energía energy (8A)

enérgico/a energetic (1B)

enero January (1B)

enfermarse to get sick (7A)

enfermedad *f.* sickness; disease

enfermero/a *n.* nurse (7A)

enfermo/a *n.* sick person; *adj.* sick; **estar** (*irreg.*) **enfermo/a** to be sick (7A)

enfoque *m.* focus

enfrentarse a to face, confront

enfrente de across from (2A); in front of (2A)

engañador(a) deceitful (7B)

engañar to deceive (7B); to cheat on (7B)

engañoso/a deceitful

enlace *m.* link (5A)

enlatado/a canned

enojado/a angry (5B)

enojarse to get mad (7A)

enorme enormous

ensalada salad; **ensalada mixta** tossed salad (3B)

enseñanza teaching (9B)

enseñar to teach (1A)

entender (ie) to understand (2A)

enterarse de to find out about

entero/a entire, whole; **limpiar la casa entera** to clean the whole house (4B)

enterrar (ie) to bury

entonces then

entrada entrance; ticket

entrante: la semana entrante next week (1B)

entrar (**en** + *place*) to enter (*a place*)

entre between (1B)

entregar (gu) to hand in

entrelazar (c) to intertwine

entrenamiento training

entrenar to train (9A)

entretanto meanwhile

entretener (*like* **tener**) to entertain (8B)

entretenido/a amused, entertained, fun (8B)

entretenimiento entertainment, amusement

entrevista interview; **programa** (*m.*) **de entrevistas** talk show (8B)

entrevistar to interview

entrometerse to meddle

entrometido/a meddlesome

entusiasmado/a enthusiastic; excited

enviar (envío) to send (5A)

envidia envy; **tenerle** (*irreg.*) **envidia (a alguien)** to be envious (of someone) (7A)

envidioso/a envious (9A)

episodio episode

época era, age

equilibrado/a well-balanced

equipado/a equipped

equipaje *m.* luggage (6A); **facturar el equipaje** to check luggage (6A)

equipo team (4A); **trabajar en equipo** to work as a team (9A)

equivalente equivalent

equivaler (*like* **valer**) to be equivalent; to be equal

equivocarse (qu) to be mistaken

error *m.* error, mistake

erupción *f.* eruption

escala scale; ladder; layover; **hacer** (*irreg.*) **escala** to make a stopover (6A)

escalada: practicar (qu) la escalada to rappel

escalar montañas to go mountain climbing

escalofríos *pl.* chills; **darle** (*irreg.*) **escalofríos a alguien** to give someone chills (7B)

escandaloso/a scandalous (8B)

escapar (de) to escape (from) (8B)

escasez (*pl.* **escaseces**) *f.* scarcity

escena scene
esclavo/a slave
escoba broom (4B)
escoger (j) to choose
escoliosis *f.* scoliosis
esconder to hide
escondite (*m.*): **jugar (ue) (gu) al escondite** to play hide and seek (5A)
escorpión *m.* scorpion
escribir (*p.p.* **escrito/a**) to write (1B)
escrito/a (*p.p. of* **escribir**) written
escritor(a) writer
escritorio desk (P)
escuchar to listen (to) (1A)
escuela school (2A); **escuela secundaria** high school
escultor(a) sculptor (9B)
escultura sculpture
escurrir to drain
ese/a *adj.* that (2B); *pron.* that (one) (2B)
eso *neut. pron.* that (2B)
esos/esas *adj.* those (2B); *pron.* those (ones) (2B)
espacio space; **respetar el espacio personal** to respect personal space (9A)
espaguetis *m. pl.* spaghetti (3B)
espalda back (*of a person*) (7A); **hablar a espaldas de alguien** to talk behind someone's back (9A)
espantoso/a scary
español *n. m.* Spanish (*language*) (P)
español(a) *n.* Spaniard; *adj.* Spanish; **tortilla española** *omelette made of eggs, potatoes, and onions* (3B)
espárragos *pl.* asparagus (3B)
especial special
especialidad *f.* specialty
especialista specialist (9B)
especialización *f.* specialization, major
especie *f. s.* species; **especies en peligro de extinción** endangered species (6B)
específico/a specific
espectáculo spectacle, sight; show; **mundo de los espectáculos** entertainment industry (8A); **ver** (*irreg.*) **un espectáculo** to see a show (6B)
espejo mirror (4B)
espera: sala de espera waiting room (6A)
esperanza hope (7B)
esperar to hope; to wait for
espinacas *pl.* spinach
espíritu *m.* spirit
esponja sponge (4B)
espontáneo/a spontaneous (7B)
esposo/a husband, wife (3A); *pl.* married couple
espuma foam
esquiar (esquío) (en el agua) to (water) ski (4A)

esquina corner (*street*)
estable *adj.* stable (5B)
establecer (zc) to establish (5B)
establecimiento establishment
estación *f.* season (1B); station; **estación del tren** train station (2A)
estacionar to park
estacionario stationary; **hacer** (*irreg.*) **ciclismo estacionario** to ride a stationary bike (4A)
estadio stadium (2A)
estado *n.* state; condition; **estado físico** physical condition (7A); **Estado Libre Asociado** Free Associated State, Commonwealth; **Estados Unidos** United States
estadounidense *n., adj.* of or from the United States
estallar to explode
estampilla stamp; **coleccionar estampillas** to collect stamps (4A)
estanco tobacco shop (2A)
estante *m.* bookshelf (4B)
estantería *s.* shelves, bookcase
estar *irreg.* to be (P); **está despejado** it's clear (*weather*) (1B); **está lloviendo** it's raining (1B); **está nevando** it's snowing (1B); **está nublado** it's cloudy (1B); **estar a buen precio** to be a good price; **estar a nombre de...** to be in...'s name; **estar al corriente** to be caught up (*with current events*) (8B); **estar celoso/a** to be jealous (7A); **estar de acuerdo** to agree; **estar en (buena) forma** to be in (good) shape (4A); **estar enfermo/a** to be sick (7A); **estar listo/a** to be ready; **estar por** + *inf.* to be about to (*do something*); **estar seguro/a de** to be sure of (8B); **estoy buscando...** I'm looking for ... (2B); **sólo estoy mirando** I'm just looking (2B)
estatua statue
estatura: de estatura mediana of medium height (3A)
estatus *m.* status
este *m.* east; **al este de** to the east of (2A)
este/a *adj.* this (2B); *pron.* this (one) (2B); **esta noche** tonight (1B)
este... uh ... (*pause sound*)
estelar: hora estelar prime time
estéreo (portátil) (portable) stereo (5A)
estereotipado/a stereotyped
estereotipo *n.* stereotype
estilo style
estimar to think highly of (7B)
estimulante stimulating (1B)
estimular to stimulate
estímulo stimulus
esto *neut. pron.* this (2B)
estómago stomach (7A)

estos/as *adj.* these (2B); *pron.* these (ones) (2B)
estrategia strategy
estratégico/a strategic
estrecho/a close
estrella star
estrenar to debut
estreno debut
estrés *m.* stress; **sufrir de estrés** to suffer from stress
estresado/a stressed
estricto/a strict
estrofa verse
estructura structure
estructural structural
estudiante *m., f.* student (P)
estudiantil *adj.* student; **centro estudiantil** student center/union (2A); **residencia estudiantil** dormitory (P)
estudiar to study (1A); **estudio...** I study ..., I'm studying ... (P); **¿qué estudias?** what are you (*fam. s.*) studying?
estudio study; *pl.* studies, schooling; **estudios de posgrado** graduate studies (9B); **estudios interdepartamentales** interdisciplinary studies (P); **estudios latinos** Latino studies (P); **estudios sobre el género** gender studies (P)
estudioso/a studious
estufa stove (4B)
estupendo/a stupendous
estupidez *f.* (*pl.* **estupideces**) stupid thing
etapa step, stage
ética *s.* ethics
etiope *adj. m., f.* Ethiopian
etiqueta etiquette
etnicidad *f.* ethnicity
étnico/a ethnic
etnografía ethnography, study of the races of people
Europa Europe (6B)
europeo/a *adj.* European
evaluación *f.* evaluation
evaluar (evalúo) to evaluate
evento event
evidencia evidence
evidente evident
evitar to avoid
evolucionar to evolve
exacto/a exact
exageración *f.* exaggeration
exagerado/a exaggerated (8B)
exagerar to exaggerate (8B)
examen *m.* test; **examen médico** medical exam (7A)
examinar to examine (7A)
excavación *f.* excavation
excelencia excellence
excelente excellent

excéntrico/a eccentric (1B)
excepción f. exception
excepcional exceptional
excepto adv. except
excesivo/a excessive
excluir (y) to exclude
exclusivo/a exclusive
excursión f. excursión; **ir** (irreg.) **de excursión** to go on a hike, go hiking (6B)
excusa excuse
exhibir to exhibit
exigencias pl. demands
exigente demanding
exigir (j) to demand
exilado/a exiled
exilio exile
existir to exist
éxito success (5B); **tener** (irreg.) **éxito** to be successful (5B)
exitoso/a successful
exótico/a exotic; strange
expandir to expand
expansión f. expansion
expectativa expectation (9A); **tener** (irreg.) **expectativas** to have expectations
expedir (i, i) to expedite; to issue
experiencia n. experience
experimentar to test, try out; to experience
experimento experiment
experto/a n., adj. expert
explicación f. explanation
explicar (qu) to explain
exploración f. exploration (5B)
explorador(a) explorer
explorar to explore (5B)
explosión f. explosion
explosivo/a explosive (1B)
explotar to exploit
exponer (like **poner**) to expose, report
exportación f. exportation; **productos de exportación** export products (8A)
exportador(a) exporter
exportar to export (8A)
expresar to express
expresión f. expression
expulsado/a expelled; thrown out
expulsar to eject
exquisito/a exquisite
extender (ie) to extend
extendido/a extended; **familia extendida** extended family (3A)
extensión f. extension
exterior m. exterior
extinción f. extinction; **especies** (f. pl.) **en peligro de extinción** endangered species (6B)
extranjero n. abroad; **ir** (irreg.) **al extranjero** to go abroad (6A)

extranjero/a n. foreigner; adj. foreign
extrañar to miss (someone) (7B); to be strange
extraño/a strange
extraordinario/a extraordinary
extraviar (extravío) to lose (something)
extremista n., adj. m., f. extremist
extremo n. extreme
extrovertido/a extroverted (1B)

F

fábrica factory (6B)
fabricado/a manufactured; **bienes** (m. pl.) **fabricados** manufactured goods (8A)
fabricar (qu) to make
fácil easy
facilidad f. ease; facility
facilitar to facilitate, make easy
factor m. factor, cause
facturar el equipaje to check luggage (6A)
facultad f. department (P)
falda skirt (2B)
falla error
falsificado/a falsified
falso/a false
falta n. lack (6B)
faltar to be missing, lacking
familia family (3A); **familia extendida** extended family (3A); **visitar a la familia** to visit one's family (1A)
familiar adj. pertaining to a family
famoso/a famous
fanático/a fan, enthusiast
fantástico/a fantastic
farmacéutico/a n. pharmacist (7A); adj. pharmaceutical; **producto farmacéutico** pharmaceutical product (8A)
farmacia pharmacy (2A)
fascinante fascinating
fascinar to love, be fascinated by (5A)
fatal awful
fatiga fatigue
favor m. favor; **hacerle** (irreg.) **un favor a alguien** to do someone a favor (9A); **por favor** please
favorecer (zc) to favor
favorito/a favorite
fax m.: **máquina fax** fax machine (5A)
febrero February (1B)
fecha date (calendar) (5B)
federal: distrito federal federal district
felicidad f. happiness
felicitación f. congratulations; **tarjeta de felicitación** greeting card
felicitar to congratulate
feliz (pl. **felices**) happy (5B)
femenino/a feminine
fenómeno phenomenon

feo/a ugly (3A)
fertilizante m. fertilizer
festivo: día (m.) **festivo** holiday (4A)
fiar (fío) to trust; **(no) ser** (irreg.) **de fiar** to be (un)reliable (9A)
ficción f. fiction; **ciencia ficción** science fiction
fiebre f. fever; **tener** (irreg.) **fiebre** to have a fever (7A)
fiel faithful (7B)
fiesta party (4A); **dar** (irreg.) **una fiesta** to throw a party (4A); **Fiesta de las Luces** Hanukkah (4A); **fiesta de sorpresa** surprise party (4A)
fiestero/a fond of parties
figura figure
fijar to arrange, set up; **fijarse en** to take note of, notice
fijo/a fixed; **precio fijo** fixed price (2B)
filete m. fillet
filmación f. filming
filmar to film
filosofía philosophy (P)
filosófico/a philosophical
fin m. end; **con fines de lucro** for profit; **fin de semana** weekend (1A); **poner** (irreg.) **fin a** to end; **por fin** finally
final m. end; adj. final
finalizar (c) to finalize
finanzas (pl.) **personales** personal finances (8A)
firmar to sign (4B)
física s. physics (P)
físico/a physicist (9B); **estado físico** physical condition (7A)
flagrante flagrant
flan m. flan (baked custard) (3B)
flexible flexible (9A)
flor f. flower
florecer (zc) to flourish
florido/a flowery; **Pascua Florida** Easter (4A)
fluvial adj. related to rivers
fólico: ácido fólico folic acid
folleto brochure
fondo fund
forestal adj. forest
forjar to create
forma form, shape; **estar** (irreg.) **en (buena) forma** to be in (good) shape (4A)
formación f. formation
formar to form
formato format
foro forum
fortalecer (zc) to strengthen (4A)
fortuna luck
forzado/a forced
fósil m. fossil; **combustibles** (m.) **fósiles** fossil fuels (6B)
foto picture; **sacar (qu) fotos** to take pictures

foto(grafía) photo(graph); photography

fotografiado/a photographed

fotógrafo/a photographer (9B)

fracasar to fail (5B)

fracaso failure (5B)

frágil fragile

francamente frankly

francés *m.* French (*language*) (P)

francés, francesa *n., adj.* French

franja strip (*of land*)

frase *f.* phrase

frecuencia frecuency; **con frecuencia** frequently

frecuente frequent

fregar (ie) (gu) to clean (4B)

frente a *prep.* in the face of; versus; facing

fresco/a fresh cool; **hace fresco** it's cool (*weather*) (1B)

frijol *m.* bean

frío *n.:* **hace (mucho) frío** it's (very) cold (*weather*) (1B)

frío/a *adj.* cold

frito/a (*p.p. of* **freír**) fried; **huevo frito** fried egg (3B); **papas fritas** French fries (3B)

frontera border

frustración *f.* frustration

frustrado/a frustrated (7A)

frustrar(se) to frustrate (7A)

fruta fruit (3B); **barra de frutas** fruit bar (3B)

frutería fruit store

fuego fire; **arma** (*f.* [*but* **el arma**]) **de fuego** firearm

fuente *f.* source; fountain

fuera de outside (of); **por fuera** (on the) outside

fuerte strong (4A)

fuerza strength

fumar to smoke

función *f.* function

funcionar to function, work (*machines*) (5A)

fundación *f.* foundation; founding (5B)

fundamental basic

funicular *m.* funicular, railway

furioso/a furious (7A)

fusilamiento shooting

fútbol *m.* soccer (4A); **fútbol americano** football (4A)

futbolista *m., f.* soccer player

futuro *n.* future

futuro/a *adj.* future

G

gallego Galician (*language spoken in the region of Galicia in northwest Spain*)

galleta cookie (3B); **galleta salada** cracker (3B)

gallina hen (9A); **ponérsele** (*irreg.*) **la piel de gallina a alguien** to get goosebumps (7B)

gamba shrimp (*Sp.*)

ganador(a) winner

ganancias *pl.* earnings

ganar to win (4A); to earn (8A)

ganas *pl.:* **tener** (*irreg.*) **ganas de** + *inf.* to feel like (*doing something*)

ganga bargain (2B)

garaje *m.* garage (4B)

garantizar (c) to guarantee

garganta throat (7A)

gárgaras *pl.:* **hacer** (*irreg.*) **gárgaras** to gargle

gasolina gasoline

gastar to spend (2B)

gastos *pl.* expenses (8A)

gastronomía gastronomy, cuisine

gato/a cat (3A)

gemelo/a twin (3A)

gemir (i, i) to groan, moan (9A); to howl (9A)

genealógico/a genealogical; **árbol** (*m.*) **genealógico** family tree

generación *f.* generation

general: en general in general

generalización *f.* generalization

generar to generate

genérico/a generic

género gender; genre; **estudios sobre el género** gender studies (P)

generoso/a generous (7B)

gente *f. s.* people; **rozarse (c) con la gente** to mingle with people (4A); **tener** (*irreg.*) **don de gentes** to have a way with people (9B)

geografía geography

geográfico/a geographical

geometría geometry

gerente *m., f.* manager

gesto gesture

gimnasia: hacer (*irreg.*) **gimnasia** to work out (4A)

gimnasio gymnasium (2A)

globalizado/a globalized

gobernador(a) governor

gobierno government (8B)

golf *m.* golf (4A)

golfo gulf (6B)

gordito/a chubby (3A)

gordo/a fat

gorra baseball cap (2B)

gozar (c) de to enjoy

grabar to record (5A)

gracias thank you; **dar** (*irreg.*) **las gracias** to thank; **Día** (*m.*) **de Acción de Gracias** Thanksgiving (4A)

gracioso/a funny (8B)

graduación *f.* graduation (5B)

graduarse (me gradúo) to graduate (5B)

gramática grammar

gran, grande large, big (1B); great (1B); **creo que le queda un poco grande** I think it's a bit big on you (2B); **Gran Bretaña** Great Britain

granola: barra de granola granola bar (3B)

grasa *n.* fat

grasoso/a greasy

gratis *adv. inv.* free (*of charge*)

grave serious

gregario/a gregarious (1B)

grifo tap, faucet; **agua** (*m.*) **del grifo** tap water

gris gray (2B)

gritar to yell, shout (9A)

grosero/a rude

grueso/a thick

grupo group

guapo/a handsome (3A); good-looking (3A)

guaraní *m.* Guarani (*indigenous language of Paraguay*)

guardar (documentos) to keep, save (documents) (5A); **guardar(le) rencor (a alguien)** to hold a grudge (against someone) (7B)

guatemalteco/a *n., adj.* Guatemalan

guerra war (5B); **guerra civil** civil war; **Guerra Fría** Cold War

guía *m., f.* guide (*person*); *f.* guidebook

guiar (guío) to guide

guisante *m.* pea

guitarra guitar; **tocar (qu) la guitarra** to play the guitar (1A)

gustar(le) to be pleasing (*to someone*) (3B); **me gusta...** I like ... (1A); **te gusta...** you (*fam. s.*) like ... (1A)

gusto taste; pleasure; **mucho gusto** pleased to meet you (P)

H

haber *irreg.* to have (*aux.*)

habichuela bean

hábil skillful; proficient; **ser** (*irreg.*) **hábil para (las matemáticas, las ciencias)** to be good at (math, science) (9B)

habilidad *f.* ability; skill

habitación *f.* (dorm) room (2A)

habitante *m., f.* inhabitant

habitar to live

hablante *m., f.* speaker

hablar to speak (1A); **hablar a espaldas de alguien** to talk behind someone's back (9A)

hacer *irreg.* (*p.p.* **hecho/a**) to make (2A); to do (2A); **hace** + *time* *time* ago (7A); **hace** + *time* + **que** + *present* it's been (*time*) since . . . ; **hace (mucho tiempo)** (a long time) ago; **hace... años** . . . years ago; **hace**

buen/mal tiempo it's good/bad weather (1B); **hace (mucho) calor/frío** it's (very) hot/cold (1B); **hace fresco** it's cool (*weather*) (1B); **hace sol** it's sunny (1B); **hace (mucho) viento** it's (very) windy (1B); **hacer autostop** to hitchhike; **hacer camping** to go camping (6B); **hacer ciclismo estacionario** to ride a stationary bike (4A); **hacer clic** to click (5A); **hacer cola** to stand in line (6A); **hacer ejercicio** to exercise (4A); **hacer ejercicio aeróbico** to do aerobics (4A); **hacer el salto bungee** to bungee jump (6B); **hacer escala** to make a stopover (*on a flight*) (6A); **hacer gárgaras** to gargle; **hacer gimnasia** to work out (4A); **hacer kayak** to kayak (6B); **hacer la cama** to make the bed (4B); **hacer la maleta** to pack a suitcase (6A); **hacer las paces con** to make up with (7B); **hacer novillos** to skip/cut school (5A); **hacer rafting** to go rafting (6B); **hacer trucos** to do tricks (9A); **hacer un viaje** to take a trip (6A); **hacer una búsqueda** to do a search (5A); **hacer *zapping*** to channel surf (5A); **hacerle un favor a alguien** to do someone a favor (9A); **hacerse cargo de** to take charge (*of something*); **¿qué carrera haces?** what's your (*fam. s.*) major? (P)
hacia toward
hambre *f.* (*but* **el hambre**) hunger (8B); **tener** (*irreg.*) **hambre** to be hungry
hamburguesa hamburger (3B)
hámster *m.* hamster (9A)
hasta *prep.* until; **de las... hasta las...** from (*hour*) to (*hour*) (1A); **hasta luego** until (see you) later; **hasta que** *conj.* until (9B)
hay (*from* **haber**): **(no) hay** there is/are (not) (P); **hay que** + *inf.* it's necessary + *inf.* (2B)
hechicero/a *adj.* magic; bewitching
hecho *n.* fact; **de hecho** in fact
hecho/a (*p.p. of* **hacer**) made; done
helado *n.* ice cream (3B); **té** (*m.*) **helado** iced tea (3B)
hemisferio hemisphere
hepatitis *f.* hepatitis
heredar to inherit
herencia heritage; inheritance
herida *n.* wound
hermanastro/a stepbrother, stepsister (3A)
hermandad (*f.*) **de mujeres** sorority
hermano/a brother, sister (3A); **medio/a hermano/a** half brother, half sister (3A); *m. pl.* siblings

herramienta tool
hídrico/a of or related to water
hierba herb; grass
hígado liver (7A)
hijastro/a stepson, stepdaughter (3A)
hijo/a son, daughter (3A); **hijo/a único/a** only child (3A); *m. pl.* children
hipertensión *f.* hypertension
hipoteca mortgage (8A); **amortizar (c) una hipoteca** to pay off a mortgage (8A)
hipotético/a hypothetical
hispano/a *n., adj.* Hispanic
Hispanoamérica Latin America
hispanohablante *m., f.* Spanish speaker
historia story; history (P)
histórico/a historical
historieta anecdote; short story; tale
hogar *m.* home (4B)
hoja leaf; sheet of paper; **hoja de papel aparte** separate piece of paper
¡hola! hello! hi! (P)
hombre *m.* man (P); **hombre de negocios** businessman (9B)
hombro shoulder (7A)
homenaje *m.* homage
homicidio homicide
homogéneo/a homogeneous
honesto/a honest, sincere (1B)
honor *m.* honor
hora hour; time; **a la misma hora** at the same time (1A); **¿a qué hora... ?** at what time... ? (1A); when... ? (1A); **con dos horas de anticipación** two hours ahead of time; **¿qué hora es?** what time is it? (1A); **¿tiene Ud. la hora?** do you (*form. s.*) have the time? (1A); **¿tienes la hora?** do you (*fam. s.*) have the time? (1A)
horario schedule (1A)
hormiga ant
horno stove (4B); **al horno** baked (3B)
horrible terrible, horrible
hospital *m.* hospital (2A)
hostilidad *f.* hostility
hotel *m.* hotel (2A)
hoy en día nowadays; **¿qué día es hoy?** what day is today? (1A)
hueso bone (7A)
huésped(a) guest
huevo egg (3B); **huevo frito** fried egg (3B); **huevos revueltos** scrambled eggs (3B)
humanidades *f., pl.* humanities (P)
humano human
humano/a *adj.* human; **derechos humanos** human rights (8B)
humilde humble (1B)
humillación *f.* humiliation
humo smoke

humor *m.* humor; mood; **estar** (*irreg.*) **de buen/mal humor** to be in a good/bad mood
huracán *m.* hurricane (5B)

I

Ibérico/a: Península Ibérica Iberian Peninsula
ida: de ida one-way (6A); **de ida y vuelta** round-trip (6A)
idea idea; **es buena idea** it's a good idea (2B)
identificar (qu) to identify; **identificarse con** to identify with
idioma *m.* language (P)
iglesia church (2A)
igual equal; **al igual que** just like
igualmente likewise, same here (P)
ilegal illegal
imagen *f.* (*pl.* **imágenes**) image (8B)
imaginar to imagine
imaginario/a imaginary
imaginativo/a imaginative (1B)
impaciente impatient (5A)
impactar to have an impact
impacto *n.* impact
imperfecto *gram.* imperfect (tense)
imperio empire
impermeable *m.* raincoat (2B)
importado/a *n.* imported
importancia importance
importante important
importar to matter; to be important (5A); **importarle un pito** not to care about
imposible impossible; **es imposible** it's impossible (8B)
impresión *f.* impression
imprimir to print
impuesto *n.* tax (8B)
impulsivo/a impulsive
impulso impulse
inadecuado/a inadequate
inanimado/a inanimate
inapropiado/a inappropriate (8B)
inca *n. m., f.* Inca
incaico/a Incan
incendio fire; **seguro contra incendios** fire insurance (8A)
incertidumbre *f.* uncertainty
incluir (y) to include
incluso/a including
incompleto/a incomplete
incontrolable uncontrollable
inconveniente inconvenient
incorporar to incorporate
increíble incredible, unbelievable
indefinido/a indefinite
independencia independence (5B)
independiente independent

independizarse (c) to become independent
indicador *m.* indicator
indicar (qu) to indicate
indiferencia indifference
indiferente indifferent (1B)
indígena *n. m., f.* indigenous (person); *adj. m., f.* indigenous, native
indigenismo indigenism
indio/a *n.* Indian
indirecto/a indirect
indiscreto indiscreet (1B)
indispensable essential
indómito/a untamed
indudablemente undoubtedly
industria industry
inesperado/a unexpected
inestabilidad *f.* instability
inestable unstable
infarto (cardíaco) heart attack
infiel *adj. m., f.* unfaithful
infierno hell
infinitivo/a *gram.* infinitive
inflación *f.* inflation (8A)
inflexión *f.* inflection
influencia influence
influir (y) en to influence
información *f.* information
informado/a informed
informarse to inform oneself (8B)
informática computer science (P)
informativo/a informative (8B)
informe *m.* report
infraestructura infrastructure
infringir (j) to infringe
infundado/a unfounded
ingeniería (civil/eléctrica/mecánica) (civil/electrical/mechanical) engineering (P)
ingeniero/a (civil, eléctrico/a, mecánico/a) (civil, electrical, mechanical) engineer (9B)
ingenuo/a naive (1B)
Inglaterra England
inglés *n. m.* English (*language*) (P)
inglés, inglesa *adj.* English
ingresos *pl.* income (8A)
inicial *adj.* initial
iniciar to initiate, begin
inmediatamente immediately
inmigración *f.* (ilegal) (illegal) immigration (8B)
inmigrante *m., f.* immigrant (5B)
inmobiliaria: agente (*m., f.*) **de inmobiliaria** real estate agent
inmóvil unmoving
inmunodeficiencia: SIDA (síndrome (*m.*) **de inmunodeficiencia adquirida)** AIDS (Acquired Immune Deficiency Syndrome) (8B)
inodoro toilet (4B)

inolvidable unforgettable
inquieto/a restless
inquilino/a tenant (4B)
insecto insect
inseguridad *f.* insecurity
inseguro/a insecure
insistir en to insist on (8B)
insolación *f.* heat stroke
inspirar to inspire
instalaciones *f. pl.* facilities
instalar to install; **instalarse en** to settle into (*a house*) (9B)
instantáneo/a: mensajero instantáneo instant messenger
instituto institute
instrucción *f.* instruction
insuficiente insufficient
integración *f.* integration
integridad *f.* integrity
inteligencia intelligence
inteligente intelligent (1B)
intención *f.* intention
intenso/a intense
intentar to try
interacción *f.* interaction
intercambiar to exchange
intercambio *n.* exchange
interdepartamental: estudios interdepartamentales interdisciplinary studies (P)
interés *m.* interest; *pl.* interest (*finance*) (8A); **tipos de interés** interest rates (8A)
interesante interesting (1B)
interesar to interest, be interesting (5A)
interior *adj.* interior (6B)
internacional international; **noticias** (*pl.*) **internacionales** international news (8B)
internar to confine
Internet *m.* Internet (5A)
interno/a internal; **órgano interno** internal organ (7A)
interpretación *f.* interpretation
interpretar to interpret, explain
interrogativo/a interrogative
intimidad *f.* intimacy
íntimo/a intimate, private; close (*relationship*) (7B)
intoxicante poisonous; intoxicating
introducir (zc) to introduce
introvertido/a introverted (1B)
inundación *f.* flood (5B)
invadir to invade (5B)
invasión *f.* invasion (5B)
inventar to invent
invernadero greenhouse; **efecto invernadero** greenhouse effect (6B)
inversión *f.* investment (8A)
invertir (ie, i) to invest (8A)
investigación *f.* research
investigador(a) researcher

investigar (gu) to research
invierno winter (1B)
invitado/a guest
invitar to invite
inyección *f.* injection; **ponerle** (*irreg.*) **una inyección (a alguien)** to give (someone) a shot (7A)
ir *irreg.* to go (1B); **ir a** to go to (1B); **ir a un concierto** to go to a concert (6B); **ir a un parque de diversiones** to go to an amusement park (6B); **ir al cine** to go to the movies; **ir al extranjero** to go abroad (6A); **ir de excursión** to go on a hike, go hiking (6B)
irresponsable irresponsible (8A)
irritado/a irritated (7A)
irritante irritating, annoying
irritar(se) to irritate (get irritated) (7A)
isla island (6B)
italiano/a *n., adj.* Italian
izquierda *n.* left-hand side; **a la izquierda de** to the left of (2A); **doblar a la izquierda** to turn left

J

jabón *m.* soap (4B)
jamás never, not ever (3B)
jamón *m.* ham (3B)
japonés, japonesa *n., adj.* Japanese
jarabe *m.* (para la tos) (cough) syrup
jardín *m.* garden (4B)
jefe/a boss, chief
jerga slang, jargon
jitomate *m.* tomato (*Mex.*)
jornada work day; **de media jornada** part-time
joven *n. m., f.* (*pl.* **jóvenes**) young person (5A); *adj.* young
joya jewel
joyería jewelry store
jubilado/a retired
jubilarse to retire (9B)
judías verdes green beans (3B)
judío/a: pascua de los judíos Passover (4A)
juego game (4A); **juego de charadas** charades
jueves *m. inv.* Thursday (1A)
juez(a) (*m. pl.* **jueces**) judge (9B)
jugador(a) player
jugar (ue) (gu) to play (2A); **jugar a los videojuegos** to play video games (5A); **jugar al escondite** to play hide and seek (5A)
jugo juice (3B)
julio July (1B)
junio June (1B)
junto/a together
jurado panel of judges
jurar to swear (*an oath*) (9B)

justificar (qu) to justify
justo/a *adj.* fair (9A)
juvenil *adj.* youth
juventud *f.* youth (5A)
juzgar (gu) to judge (9A)

K

kayak: hacer (*irreg.*) **kayak** to kayak (6B)
kilo(grama) *m.* kilogram
kilómetro kilometer (4A)

L

la *f. def. art.* the (P); *d.o.* her, it, you (*f. form. s.*); **a la una** at one o'clock (1A); **es la una** it's one o'clock (1A)
labio lip
laboratorio laboratory
lacio/a: pelo lacio straight hair (3A)
lácteo/a dairy; **producto lácteo** dairy product (3B)
lado *n.* side; **al lado de** beside (2A)
ladrillo brick
lago lake (6B)
lamer to lick (9A)
lámpara lamp (4A)
lana wool (2B)
langosta lobster (3B)
lanza: punta de lanza spearhead
lanzar (c) to throw, fling; **lanzarse** to break into (*career*)
lápiz *m.* (*pl.* **lápices**) pencil (P)
largo/a long (3A); **a lo largo de** throughout; **de largo plazo** long-term
las *f. pl.* the (P); *d.o.* you (*f. form. pl.*); them; **a las...** at ... o'clock (1A)
lástima compassion; shame; **lástima que...** too bad that ...
lastimar(se) to hurt (oneself) (7A)
lata de aluminio aluminum can (6B)
latino/a *adj.* Latino, Latina; **estudios latinos** Latino studies (P)
Latinoamérica Latin America
latinoamericano/a *n., adj.* Latin American
lavabo sink (bathroom) (4B)
lavadora washing machine (4B)
lavaplatos *m. inv.* dishwasher (4B)
lavar to wash (4B); **lavarse los dientes** to brush one's teeth (5A)
le *i.o. s.* to/for him, her, it, you (*form. s.*)
leal loyal (1B)
lealtad *f.* loyalty
lección *f.* lesson
leche *f.* milk (3B); **café** (*m.*) **con leche** coffee with milk
lechuga lettuce (3B)
lector(a) reader
lectura *n.* reading
leer (y) to read (1B)

legalmente legally
legítimo/a legitimate
lejano/a distant, far
lejía *n.* bleach (4B)
lejos de *adv.* far away from (2A)
lengua tongue; language (P); **lengua extranjera** foreign language; **sacar (qu) la lengua** to stick out one's tongue (7A); **trabársele la lengua a alguien** to get tongue-tied (7B)
lenguaje *m.* language
lentes *m. pl.* glasses (*vision*)
lento/a slow
les *i.o. pl.* to/for you (*form. pl.*), them
letra letter (*of the alphabet*); lyrics; **letra cursiva** italics; *pl.* humanities
levantar to lift, raise up; **levantar pesas** to lift weights (4A); **levantarse** to get up (5A)
léxico vocabulary
ley *f.* law (8B)
leyenda legend
liberal liberal (1B)
libertad *f.* liberty, freedom (8B)
libertino/a libertine
libra pound (*weight*)
libre free (unfettered); **al aire libre** outdoors (6B); **Estado Libre Associado** Free Associated State, Commonwealth; **ratos libres** free time (4A)
librería bookstore (P)
libro book (P)
licencia license; **sacar (qu) la licencia de conducir** to get a driver's license (5A)
licor *m.* liquor
ligarse con to get together with
ligero/a *adj.* light
limitar to limit
límite *m.* limit
limón *m.* lemon (3B)
limonada lemonade
limpiar to clean; **limpiar la casa (entera)** to clean the (whole) house (4B)
limpieza *n.* cleaning; cleanliness; **producto de limpieza** cleaning product (4B)
lindo/a pretty
línea line; **línea aérea** airline; **patinar en línea** to inline skate (4A)
lingüístico/a linguistic
lío problem; **meterse en líos** to get into trouble (5A)
lista list
listo/a ready (1B); clever, smart (2B); **estar** (*irreg.*) **listo/a** to be ready; **ser** (*irreg.*) **listo/a** to be clever
literatura literature (P)
llamada *n.* (telephone) call
llamar to call (1A); **¿cómo se llama (él/ella)?** what's his/her name? (P);

¿cómo te llamas? what's your (*fam. s.*) name? (P); **llamar por teléfono** to call on the telephone (1A); **llamarse** to be called; **me llamo...** my name is . . . (P)
llanura flatland, prairie (6B)
llave *n. f.* key
llegada arrival
llegar (gu) to arrive; **¿cómo se llega a... ?** how do you get to . . . ? (6A); **llegar a tiempo** to arrive on time (1A)
llenar to fill
lleno/a full
llevar to take, carry (1A); to wear (*clothing*) (2B); **llevar al / a la veterinario/a** to take to the veterinarian (9A); **llevar... créditos** to have . . . credits (1A); **llevarse bien/mal con** to get along well/poorly with (5A)
llorar to cry (7A)
llover (ue) to rain; **está lloviendo** it's raining (1B); **llueve** it's raining (1B)
lluvia rain
lluvioso/a rainy; **bosque** (*m.*) **lluvioso** rain forest (6B)
lo *d.o.* him, it, you (*m. form. s.*); **lo que** what, that which (1B)
local local; **noticias locales** local news (8B)
localizador *m.* pager
localizarse (c) to be located
loco/a mad, crazy
lógico/a logical
lograr + *inf.* to succeed (*in doing something*) (9B)
lomo loin
longitud *f.* duration
loro parrot (9A)
los *def. art. m. pl.* the (P); *d.o.* them, you (*form. pl.*); **los años veinte (treinta)** the twenties (thirties) (5B); **los/lás demás** others (4A)
lucha *n.* fight; struggle
lucro: con fines de lucro for profit
luego then; **hasta luego** until (see you) later
lugar *m.* place (2A)
lujo luxury; **hotel** (*m.*) **de lujo** luxury hotel (6A)
lunar *m.:* **de lunares** polka-dotted (2B)
lunes *m. inv.* Monday (1A); **el (los) lunes** on Monday(s) (1A)
luz *f.* (*pl.* **luces**) light (P); electricity; **Fiesta de las Luces** Hanukkah (4A)

M

madera wood (8A)
madrastra stepmother (3A)
madre *f.* mother (3A); **madre soltera** single mother (3A)

madrina godmother

madrugada early morning hours

maestría *n.* mastery, skill; master's degree (9B)

maestro/a (de primaria, secundaria) (elementary, high school) teacher (9B)

magia *n.* magic

magos *pl.*: **los Reyes** (*m.*) **Magos** the Magi (Three Wise Men); **Día** (*m.*) **de los Reyes Magos** Epiphany (January 6), Day of the Magi

maíz *m.* corn (3B); **palomitas de maíz** popcorn (3B); **tortilla de maíz** corn tortilla (3B)

mal, malo/a *adj.* bad (1B); sick (2B); **caerle** (*irreg.*) **mal a alguien** to dislike someone (5A); **hace mal tiempo** it's bad weather (1B); **llevarse mal con** to get along poorly with (5A); **manejar mal** to manage poorly (8A); **pasarlo mal** to have a bad time (4A); **portarse mal** to misbehave (5A); **quedarle mal** to fit poorly

maldad *n. f.* evil

maleta suitcase; **hacer** (*irreg.*) **la maleta** to pack a suitcase (6A)

maletero skycap, porter (6A)

maletín *m.* briefcase

malicioso/a malicious (1B)

mamá mom; mother

mandar to send; to order (5A)

mandato *n.* command

mando a distancia remote control (5A)

mandón, mandona bossy (7B)

manejar (bien/mal) to manage (well/poorly) (8A)

manera manner, way; **pensar (ie) de manera directa** to think in a direct (linear) manner (9B)

manifestación *f.* demonstration (8B)

manifestar(se) (ie) to manifest, show

manipular to manipulate (8B)

mano *f.* hand (7A); **darse** (*irreg.*) **la mano** to shake hands (7B)

mansión *f.* mansion

mantel *m.* tablecloth

mantener (*like* **tener**) to maintain; to support; **mantenerse a raya** to keep (*something*) away

mantequilla butter (3B); **mantequilla de cacahuete** peanut butter (3B)

manual *m.* workbook

manufacturado/a manufactured

manzana apple (3B); city block (6A)

mañana *n.* morning; *adv.* tomorrow (1A); **de la mañana** in the morning (A.M.) (1A); **hasta mañana** until (see you) tomorrow; **pasado mañana** the day after tomorrow (1B); **por la mañana** in the morning (1A)

mapa *m.* map (6A)

máquina machine; **máquina fax** fax machine (5A)

mar *m., f.* sea, ocean (6B)

maravilloso/a marvelous

marca brand name (2B)

marcar (qu) to mark

mareado/a nauseated, dizzy

marearse to get nauseated, sick (*boat, car, plane*) (6A)

marido husband (3A)

marino/a *adj.* marine

mariscos *pl.* shellfish (3B); seafood (3B)

marrón *adj. m., f.* brown (2B)

martes *m. inv.* Tuesday (1A); **Martes de Carnaval** Mardi Gras (4A)

marzo March (1B)

más *adv.* more; **cada vez más** more and more; **es más** what's more; **más… que** more . . . than (3A)

mascota *n.* pet (3A)

masculino/a masculine

matar to kill

matemáticas mathematics (P)

materia subject (*school*) (P)

material *m.* material

materialista *m., f.* materialist

materno/a maternal (3A)

matrícula tuition

matrimonial: cama matrimonial queen bed (4B)

matrimonio matrimony, marriage (5B)

mayo May (1B)

mayor older (3A); **el/la mayor** the oldest

mayoría majority

me *d.o.* me; *i.o.* to/for me; *refl. pron.* myself; **me gusta…** I like . . . (1A); **me llamo** my name is (P); **me parece(n)…** it/that seems . . . to me; **¿me podría traer…?** could you (*form. s.*) bring me . . . ? (6A)

mecánico/a mechanic; **ingeniería mecánica** mechanical engineering (P); **ingeniero/a mecánico/a** mechanical engineer (9B)

media *n.* average

mediano/a *adj.* medium; average (2B); **de estatura mediana** of medium height (3A)

medianoche *f.* midnight (1A); **a medianoche** at midnight

medias *pl.* stockings (2B); pantyhose (2B)

medicación *f.* medication

medicina medicine (7A)

médico/a *n.* doctor (7A); *adj.* medical; **examen** (*m.*) **médico** medical exam (7A); **seguro médico** medical insurance (8A); **servicios médicos** medical services (9B)

medidas *pl.* measures

medio *n. s.* means, middle; **medio ambiente** environment (6B); **medios de comunicación** media (8B)

medio/a *adj.* half; middle; **clase** (*f.*) **media** middle class; **medio/a hermano/a** half brother/sister (3A); **media pensión** room and one other meal (usually breakfast) (6A); **y media** half past (*hour*) (1A)

medioambiental environmental

mediodía *m.* noon, midday (1A); **a mediodía** at noon

meditar to meditate (4A)

mediterráneo/a *adj.* Mediterranean

mejillas cheeks (3A)

mejor better (3A)

mejorar to improve

melodrama *m.* melodrama

membresía membership

memoria memory

memorizar (c) to memorize (1A)

mencionar to mention

mendigo/a beggar

menor younger (3A); **el/la menor** the youngest

menos less; least; **a menos que** *conj.* unless (7B); **menos cuarto** a quarter to (*hour*) (1A); **menos… que** less . . . than (3A); **por lo menos** at least

mensaje *m.* message (5A)

mensajero/a messenger; **mensajero instantáneo** instant messenger

mensual monthly; **presupuesto mensual** monthly budget (8A)

mentalidad *f.* mentality

mente *f.* mind

mentir (ie, i) to lie (4B)

mentira lie

mentiroso/a liar (5A)

mentón *m.* chin (3A)

menú *m.* menu (6A)

menudo: a menudo often

mercadeo marketing (9B)

mercado market (2A)

mercancías *pl.* goods

merecer (zc) to deserve (3A)

merendar (ie) to snack (3B)

meridional southern

merienda *n.* snack (3B)

mérito merit; **atribuirse (y) todo el mérito** to take all the credit (9A)

mermelada jam (3B)

mes *m.* month (1B); **cada mes** each month; **¿en qué mes cae…?** ¿what month is . . . ?; **una vez al mes** once a month (1B)

mesa table (P)

mesero/a waiter, waitress (6A)

meseta plateau (6B)

mesita end table (4B)

mestizaje *m.* mixing of races

mestizo/a *n.* mixed-race person

meta goal (9B); **alcanzar (c) una meta** to reach a goal (9B)

metales (*m.*) **preciosos** precious metals (8A)

meteorológico/a meteorological

meterse to pick a fight (9A); **meterse en líos** to get into trouble (5A)

metódico/a methodical (1B)

metro meter (4A); **metros cuadrados** square meters (4B)

mexicano/a *n., adj.* Mexican

mexicanoamericano/a *n., adj.* Mexican-American

mezcla mixture

mezquita mosque

mí *obj. of prep.* (4B)

mi(s) *poss.* my (4B); **mi apellido es...** my last name is . . . (P); **mi nombre es...** my name is . . . (P)

microondas *m. s.* microwave (4B)

microscopio microscope

miedo fear; **tener(le)** (*irreg.*) **miedo (a alguien)** to be afraid (of someone) (7A)

miembro/a member

mientras *adv.* meanwhile (5B); **mientras que** *conj.* while

miércoles *m. inv.* Wednesday (1A)

migración *f.* migration (5B)

migratorio/a migratory

mil thousand, one thousand (2B)

militar *adj.* military

milla mile (4A)

millón *m.* **(de)** million (5B)

millonario millionaire

mina *n.* mine

miniserie *f.* miniseries

minoría minority

minoritario/a *adj.* minority

minuto minute

mío/a/os/as *poss.* my, (of) mine (2B)

mirar to look (at), watch (1A); **sólo estoy mirando** I'm just looking (2B)

misceláneo/a miscellaneous

misión *f.* mission

mismo/a same; self; **a la misma hora** at the same time (1A)

misterio mystery

mitad *f.* half

mito myth

mitología mythology

mixto/a mixed; **ensalada mixta** tossed salad (3B)

mochila backpack (P)

moda fashion (2B); **de moda** in style

modelo model; *m., f.* model (*fashion*)

módem *m.* modem (5A)

modernización *f.* modernization

moderno/a modern

modesto/a modest

mojado/a wet

molestar to bother (3A)

momento moment, instant

moneda currency; coin; **coleccionar monedas** to collect coins (4A)

monitor *m.* monitor (5A)

monótono/a monotonous

montaña mountain (6B); **escalar montañas** to go mountain climbing (6B)

montar a caballo to go horseback riding (6B)

morado/a purple (2B)

mórbido/a morbid

morder (ue) to bite (9A)

moreno/a dark-skinned (3A)

morir(se) (ue, u) (*p.p.* **muerto/a**) to die (4B); **ya murió** he/she already died (3A)

moro/a *n.* Moor; *adj.* Moorish

morrón *m.* blow, bang, hit

mortalidad *f.* mortality

mosquetero: los Tres Mosqueteros The Three Musketeers

mostrador *m.* counter (*kitchen, etc.*)

mostrar (ue) to show (*something to someone*)

motivo motive, reason

motor *m.* engine, motor

mover (ue) to move (around); **moverse** to move (*houses*)

móvil: teléfono móvil cell phone

movimiento movement

mozo bellhop

muchacho/a boy, girl

mucho *adv.* a lot, much (1A)

mucho/a *adj.* much, a lot (of); **hace mucho calor** it's very hot (1B); **hace mucho frío** it's very cold (1B); **hace mucho viento** it's very windy (1B); **mucho gusto** pleased to meet you (P); **pasar mucho tiempo** to spend a lot of time (1A)

mudanza move (5B)

mudarse to move (*to another house*) (5B)

mueble *m.* piece of furniture (4B)

muerte *f.* death (4A); **pena de muerte** death penalty

muerto/a (*p.p. of* **morir**) dead

muestra example

mujer *f.* woman (P); wife (3A); **hermandad** (*f.*) **de mujeres**, sorority; **mujer de negocios** businesswoman (9B); **mujer policía** policewoman; **mujer político** (female) politician (9B); **mujer química** (female) chemist (9B); **mujer soldado** (female) soldier (9B)

mujeriego *n.* womanizer

muleta crutch

multa fee, fine

multinacional multinational

mundial *adj.* world

mundo world; **mundo de los espectáculos** entertainment industry (8A)

muñeca wrist; doll (5A)

muro wall

músculo muscle

museo museum; **visitar un museo** to visit a museum (4A)

música music (P)

músico/a musician

musulmán, musulmana *n., adj.* Muslim

muy very (1A)

N

nacer (zc) to be born (5B)

nacido/a born; **recién nacido/a** newborn baby (5B)

nacimiento birth (5B)

nación *f.* nation

nacional national; **noticias** (*pl.*) **nacionales** national news (8B); **producto nacional bruto** gross national product

nada nothing; none (3B)

nadador(a) swimmer

nadar to swim (4A)

nadie nobody, not anybody (3B)

nahuatl *m.* Nahuatl (*language of the Aztecs*)

naranja orange (*fruit*) (3B)

nariz *f.* nose (3A); **tener** (*irreg.*) **la nariz tapada** to have a stuffed-up nose (7A)

narración *f.* narration

narrar to narrate

natación *f.* swimming (4A)

nativo/a *adj.* native, indigenous

natural *adj.* natural; **ciencias naturales** natural sciences (P); **desastre** (*m.*) **natural** natural disaster (5B); **recursos naturales** natural resources (6B)

naturaleza nature (6B)

navegar (gu) (la red) to navigate; to surf (the Web) (1A); **navegar en barco** to sail (4A)

Navidad *f.* Christmas (4A)

navideño/a *adj.* Christmas

necesario/a necessary; **es necesario** it's necessary (2B)

necesidad *f.* necessity

necesitar to need (1A); **necesitar + inf.** to need to (*do something*)

neerlandés, neerlandesa *adj.* Dutch

negación *f.* negation

negar (ie) (gu) to deny (8B)

negativo/a *adj.* negative

negocio business (9B); **hombre** (*m.*) **de negocios** businessman (9B); **mujer** (*f.*) **de negocios** businesswoman (9B)

negrita: en negrita in boldface type

negro/a *adj.* black (2B)

nervioso/a nervous (5B)

nevar (ie) to snow; **está nevando** it's snowing (1B); **nieva** it's snowing (1B)

nevera freezer (4B)

ni... ni neither . . . nor

nieto/a grandson, granddaughter (3A); *pl.* grandchildren

ningún, ninguno/a *adj.* no, not any (3B)

ninguno/a *pron.* none, not any (3B)

niñero/a baby-sitter; nanny (5A)

niñez *f.* (*pl.* **niñeces**) childhood (5A)

niño/a child; boy, girl (5A)

nivel *m.* level; **nivel económico** economic level

no no; not; **no aguantar** not to be able to stand, put up with (7B); **no es cierto** it's not true (8B); **no es posible** it's not possible (8B); **no es seguro/a** it's not sure (8B); **no es verdad** it's not true (8B); **no obstante** nevertheless; **no ser de fiar** to be unreliable (9A); **todavía no sé** I still don't know (P); **ya no** no longer

noche *f.* night; **buenas noches** good night (P); **de la noche** in the evening (night); **esta noche** tonight (1B); **Noche Vieja** New Year's Eve (4A); **por la noche** in the evening (night); **todas las noches** every night (1A)

Nochebuena Christmas Eve (4A)

nocivo/a unhealthy, noxious

nocturno/a *adj.* nighttime

nombrar to name

nombre *m.* name; **estar** (*irreg.*) **a nombre de...** to be in . . . 's name; **mi nombre es...** my name is . . . (P)

nominar to nominate

norma norm

norte *m.* north; **al norte de** to the north of (2A)

Norteamérica North America (6B)

norteamericano/a *n., adj.* North American (*from the United States* or Canada)

nos *d.o.* us; *i.o.* to/for us; *refl. pron.* ourselves; **nos vemos** see you around

nosotros/as *sub. pron.* we (P); *obj. of prep.* us

nostálgico/a nostalgic (7B)

nota note

notable good

notar to note, notice

noticia piece of news; *pl.* news (8B); **noticias (internacionales, locales, nacionales)** (international, local, national) news (8B)

noticiero newscast, news show (8B)

novecientos/as nine hundred (2B)

novecientos mil nine hundred thousand (5B)

novedoso/a *adj.* novel

novela *n.* novel (1B)

novelista *m., f.* novelist

noventa ninety (2A)

noviazgo engagement (7B)

noviembre November (1B)

novillos: hacer (*irreg.*) **novillos** to skip/cut school (5A)

novio/a boyfriend, girlfriend; bride, groom (5B)

nube *f.* cloud

nublado/a cloudy; **está nublado** it's cloudy (1B)

nublar to darken

nudista *adj. m., f.* nudist

nuestro/a/os/as *poss.* our (1A)

nueve nine (1A)

nuevo/a new

nuez (*pl.* **nueces**) nut

número number (1A); **¿qué número calza?** what size shoe do you (*form. s.*) wear? (2B)

numeroso/a numerous

nunca never, not ever; **casi nunca** almost never

O

o or; **o... o** either . . . or

ó or (*used between two numbers to avoid confusion with zero*)

obedecer (zc) to obey (3A)

obediencia obedience

obediente obedient (5A)

objetividad *f.* objectivity

objetivo/a objective (8B)

objeto *n.* object

obligación *f.* obligation

obligar (gu) to obligate, require

obligatorio/a required

obra *n.* work (of art)

observación *f.* observation

observador(a) observer

obsesión *f.* obsession

obstáculo obstacle

obstante: no obstante nevertheless

obtener (*like tener*) to obtain, get

obvio/a obvious

ocasión *f.* occasion

ocasionar to cause

occidental *adj.* western

océano ocean (6B); **océano Pacífico** Pacific Ocean

ochenta eighty (2A)

ocho eight (1A)

ochocientos/as eight hundred (2B)

ochocientos mil eight hundred thousand (5B)

ocio leisure time

octubre October (1B)

ocultar(le) secretos (a alguien) to hide secrets (from someone) (7B)

ocupación *f.* occupation

ocupado/a busy

ocupar to occupy

ocurrir to occur

odiar to hate (4B)

odio hatred

oeste *m.* west; **al oeste de** to the west of (2A)

ofender(se) to offend (get offended) (7A)

ofensivo/a offensive

oferta *n.* offer

oficina office (P)

oficio job, profession; trade

ofrecer (zc) to offer (3A)

oír *irreg.* to hear (2A)

ojalá que I hope, wish that (7B)

ojo eye

oleada *n.* wave

oliva: aceite (*m.*) **de oliva** olive oil

olvidar to forget

once eleven (1A)

opción *f.* option

operación *f.* operation

opinar to think, believe

opinión *f.* opinion

oportunidad *f.* opportunity

optativo/a optional

optimista *n. m., f.* optimist; *adj.* optimistic (1B)

opuesto/a opposite

oración *f.* sentence

orden *m.* order (*chronological*); **poner** (*irreg.*) **las cosas en orden** to put things in order (4B)

ordenador *m.* computer (*Sp.*)

ordenar to order, put in order (6A)

orejas (outer) ears (3A)

orgánico/a organic

organismo organism

organización *f.* organization

organizado/a organized (1B)

organizar (c) to organize

órgano organ; **órgano interno** internal organ (7A)

orgullo pride

orgulloso/a (de) proud (of) (5B)

orientación *f.* orientation, direction

origen *m.* (*pl.* **orígenes**) origin; **¿de qué origen es/son... ?** what is/are . . . 's (national) origin?

os *d.o.* you (*fam. pl. Sp.*); *i.o.* to/for you (*fam. pl. Sp.*); *refl. pron.* yourselves (*fam. pl. Sp.*)

oscurecer (zc) to get dark

oscuro/a dark (5B)

oso *n.* bear

otoño fall (*season*) (1B)

otorgar (gu) to award

otro/a other; another (1B)

oyente *m., f.* listener

ozono ozone; **capa de ozono** ozone layer (6B)

P

paciencia patience

paciente *m., f.* patient (7A); *adj.* patient (5A)

pacífico/a peaceful (5B); **océano Pacífico** Pacific Ocean

padecer (zc) de to suffer from (7A)

padrastro stepfather (3A)

padre *m.* father (3A); *pl.* parents; **padre soltero** single father (3A)

padrino godfather; **padrino de boda** groomsman

pagar (gu) to pay (for) (1A); **pagar a plazos** to pay in installments (8A); **pagar de una vez** to pay off all at once (8A)

página page; **página web** Web page (5A)

pago payment

país *m.* country (2A); **país desarrollado** developed country (8A); **país en vías de desarrollo** developing country; **País Vasco** Basque country; **los Países Bajos** The Netherlands

paisaje *m.* landscape (6B)

paisajista *adj. m., f.:* **arquitectura paisajista** landscape architecture

pájaro bird (9A)

palabra word

palabrota swear word

palomitas (*pl.*) **de maíz** popcorn (3B)

pampa pampa, prairie

pan *m.* bread; **pan dulce** sweet bread (*Mex.*) (3B); **pan tostado** toast (3B)

pana corduroy

panadería bakery

panceta *Arg.* bacon

panqueque *m.* pancake (3B)

pantalla screen (*movie, computer*) (P)

pantalón, pantalones *m.* pants (2B); **pantalones cortos** shorts (2B)

papa potato; **papas fritas** French fries (3B); **puré** (*m.*) **de papas** mashed potatoes (3B)

papá *m.* dad, father; daddy

papel *m.* role, part; paper; **hoja de papel aparte** separate piece of paper; **toalla de papel** paper towel (4B)

papitas *pl.* potato chips (3B)

paquete *m.* package

par *m.* pair; **un par de** a couple of

para for; in order to (1B); **para + *inf.*** in order to (*do something*) (2B); **para que** so that (7B)

paracaidismo skydiving; **practicar (qu) el paracaidismo** to skydive (6B)

parada de autobuses bus stop (2A)

paráfrasis *f.* paraphrase

paraguayo/a *n., adj.* Paraguayan

parapente *m.:* **practicar (qu) el parapente** to hang glide

parar to stop

parcial biased (8B); **ser** (*irreg.*) **parcial** to be biased (8A)

parcialidad *f.* bias

parecer (zc) to look; to seem (like) (5A); **me parece(n)...** it/that seems . . . to me; **parece ser** it seems to be, he/she seems . . . (1B); **parecerse (a)** to resemble (3A)

parecido/a (a) similar (to)

pared *f.* wall; **pintar las paredes** to paint the walls (4B)

pareja couple (7B); mate; partner; *pl.* pairs

paréntesis *m. inv.* parenthesis

pariente *m., f.* relative (3A)

parque *m.* park (2A); **ir** (*irreg.*) **a un parque de diversiones** to go to an amusement park (6B)

párrafo paragraph

parte *f.* part; **partes del cuerpo** parts of the body (7A)

participar to participate (8B)

particular particular; private; **casa particular** private residence (4B)

partido game (4A); **partido político** political party

pasa raisin (3B)

pasado/a *adj.* past; spoiled (*food*) (3B); **pasado mañana** the day after tomorrow (1B)

pasajero/a *n.* passenger (6A)

pasaporte *m.* passport (6A)

pasar (mucho) tiempo to pass, spend (a lot of) time (1A); **pasar a ser** to become; **pasar la aspiradora** to vacuum (4B); **pasar por la aduana** to go through customs (6A); **pasar por seguridad** to go through security (6A); **pasarlo bien/mal** to have a good/bad time (4A)

pasatiempo pastime

Pascua: Pascua (de los judíos) Passover (4A); **Pascua (Florida)** Easter (4A)

pasear to walk, stroll; **sacar (qu) a pasear** to take for a walk (9A)

paseo *n.* walk, stroll; **dar** (*irreg.*) **un paseo** to take a walk (4A)

pasión *f.* passion

paso step

pastel *m.* pastry; cake (3B); *pl.* pastries (3B); **porción** (*f.*) **de pastel** slice of cake (3B)

pastilla pill (7A)

patata potato (*Sp.*)

paterno/a paternal (3A)

patinar (en línea) to (inline) skate (4A)

patio courtyard, patio (4B)

patria homeland

Patricio: Día (*m.*) **de San Patricio** St. Patrick's Day (4A)

patrio/a patriotic

pavo turkey (3B)

paz *f.* (*pl.* **paces**) peace; **dejar en paz** to leave alone; **hacer** (*irreg.*) **las paces** to make up with (7B)

peca *n.* freckle (3A)

pecado *n.* sin

pecho chest (7A); **tomarse algo muy a pecho** to take something to heart (7A); to feel something intensely (7A)

peculiaridad *f.* peculiarity

pedagogía pedagogy; education

pedazo piece

pedir (i, i) to ask for, request (2B); to order (*restaurant*) (6A); **pedir ayuda** to ask for help; **pedir disculpas** to apologize (*to someone*); **pedir prestado/a** to borrow (8A)

pegado/a stuck on; close together

peinado hairdo

peinar to comb (9A)

pelar to peel

pelearse to fight (5A)

película movie (1A); **ver** (*irreg.*) **una película** to watch a movie

peligro danger; **especies** (*f. pl.*) **en peligro de extinción** endangered species (6B)

peligroso/a dangerous

pelirrojo/a red-headed (3A)

pelo (canoso/lacio/rizado/rubio) (gray/straight/curly/blond) hair (3A)

pelotero/a: ser (*irreg.*) **pelotero/a** to be a kiss-up (9A)

pena shame; penalty; sorrow; **pena de muerte** death penalty

península Ibérica Iberian Peninsula

pensar (ie) to think (2A); **pensar de** to think of; **pensar de manera directa** to think in a direct (linear) manner (9B); **pensar en** to think about

pensión *f.* boardinghouse (6A); **media pensión** room and one other meal (usually breakfast) (6A); **pensión completa** room and all meals (6A)

peor worse (3A)

pepino (de mar) (sea) cucumber

pequeñeces *f. pl.* little things

pequeño/a little, small (2B)

per cápita: renta per cápita per capita income

perder (ie) to lose (2A); **perder peso** to lose weight

pérdida loss; **pérdida de tiempo** waste of time (8B); **pérdida de valores tradicionales** loss of traditional values (8B)

perdón *m.* forgiveness

perdonable forgivable

perdonar to forgive (7B); to pardon, excuse

perezoso/a lazy (9A)
perfeccionista *m., f.* perfectionist
perfecto/a perfect
perfil *m.* profile
periférico peripheral device
periódico newspaper (1B)
periodista *m., f.* journalist (9B)
permiso permission
permitir to allow (8B)
pero but (1A)
perpetuar (perpetúo) to perpetuate
perplejo/a perplexed (7A); **dejar perplejo/a (a alguien)** to leave (someone) perplexed
perro dog (3A)
persistente persistent
persona person (1B)
personaje *m.* character (*fictional*)
personal personal; **finanzas personales** personal finances (8A); **respetar el espacio personal** to respect personal space (9A)
personalidad *f.* personality (1B)
perspectiva perspective
pertenecer (zc) to belong
peruano/a Peruvian
pesa weight; **levantar pesas** to lift weights (4A)
pesado/a heavy
pesar(se) to weigh (oneself); **a pesar de** *prep.* in spite of, despite
pescado fish (*food*) (3B)
pescar (qu) to fish (6B)
pesimista *n. m., f.* pessimist; *adj.* pessimistic (1B)
peso weight; **bajar de peso** to lose weight; **perder (ie) peso** to lose weight
pesquero/a *adj.* fishing
pesticida pesticide (6B)
petróleo petroleum (oil) (6B)
pez *m.* (*pl.* peces) fish (*alive*) (9A)
piano piano; **tocar (qu) el piano** to play the piano (1A)
picante hot, spicy (3B)
picar (qu) to bite (9A); to nibble (4A)
picoso/a spicy (3B)
pie *m.* foot (7A); **a pie** on foot; **dedo del pie** toe (7A); **pies cuadrados** square feet (4B)
piel *f.* skin (3A); **ponérsele** (*irreg.*) **la piel de gallina a alguien** to get goosebumps (7B)
pierna leg (7A)
pijama *m. s.* pajamas (2B)
pila (recargable) (rechargeable) battery
piloto/a pilot
pinchado/a: rueda pinchada flat tire
pintar to paint (4A); **pintar las paredes** to paint the walls (4B)
pintor(a) painter (9B)
pintoresco/a picturesque

pirámide *f.* pyramid
piscina swimming pool (4A)
piso floor (4B); flat, apartment (*Sp.*) (4B); **barrer el piso** to sweep the floor (4B)
pista track (4A)
pito: importarle un pito not to care about
pizarra chalkboard (P)
pizza pizza (3B); **porción** (*f.*) **de pizza** slice of pizza (3B)
placer *m.* pleasure
plancha iron (4B)
planchar (la ropa) to iron (the clothes) (4B)
planear to plan
planeta *m.* planet
planificación *f.* planning
plano city map (6A)
planta plant (4B); floor (*of a building*) (*Sp.*) (4B)
plástico plastic; **botella de plástico** plastic bottle (6B)
plátano banana
plato plate (6A); prepared dish; *pl.* dishes (4B); **primer (segundo, tercer) plato** first (second, third) course (6A)
playa beach (6B)
plaza square, plaza (2A)
plazo term; **de corto/largo plazo** short/long term (9B); **pagar (gu) a plazos** to pay in installments (8A)
pluma pen (P)
plumero feather duster (4B)
población *f.* population
poblado/a populated
pobre *adj.* poor (1B)
pobreza poverty (8A); **umbral** (*m.*) **de la pobreza** poverty line
poco/a *adv.* little (1B); *adj.* little; *pl.* few; **dentro de poco** in a little while (1B); **un poco** a little (1B)
poder *m.* power
poder *irreg.* to be able to, can (2A); **¿en qué puedo servirle?** how may I help you (*form. s.*)? (2B); **¿me podría traer… ?** could you (*form. s.*) bring me . . . ? (6A); **¿puedo probarme… ?** may I try on . . . ? (2B)
poema *m.* poem
poemario collection of poetry
poesía poetry
poeta *m., f.* poet
polémico/a controversial
policía *f.* police force; *m.* policeman; **mujer** (*f.*) **policía** policewoman
poliéster *m.* polyester (2B)
poliomielitis *f.* polio
politeísta *adj. m., f.* polytheist, believing in more than one god
política *s.* politics (8B)
político, mujer (*f.*) **político** politician (9B)

político/a political; **ciencias políticas** political science (P); **partido político** political party
pollo chicken (3B)
polvo *n.* dust; **quitar el polvo** to dust (4B)
poner *irreg.* to put (2A); **poner alto el volumen** to turn the volume up high; **poner fin a** to end; **poner las cosas en orden** to put things in order (4B); **ponerle los cuernos (a alguien)** to be unfaithful (to someone); **ponerle una inyección (a alguien)** to give (someone) a shot (7A); **ponerse** to get, become (*emotion*); **ponerse de acuerdo** to come to an agreement; **ponérsele la piel de gallina a alguien** to get goosebumps (7B)
por for (4B); because of (4B); by, through, around; **estar** (*irreg.*) **por** + *inf.* to be about to + *inf.*; **llamar por teléfono** to call on the telephone (1A); **pasar por la aduana** to go through customs (6A); **por ciento** percent; **por dentro** within, (on the) inside; **por ejemplo** for example; **por favor** please; **por fin** finally; **por fuera** (on the) outside; **por la mañana/tarde/noche** in the morning/afternoon/evening (night) (1A); **por lo menos** at least; **por primera vez** for the first time; **¿por qué?** why? (1B); **por supuesto** of course
porcentaje *m.* percentage
porción *f.* (**de pastel, pizza**) slice (of cake, pizza) (3B)
porfiado/a persistent (7B)
porque because (1B)
portada home page (*Web*); cover (*book*)
portarse bien/mal to behave well/badly (5A)
portátil portable; **computadora portátil** laptop computer (5A); **estéreo portátil** portable stereo (5A)
portero/a doorperson (4B); building manager (4B)
portugués *m.* Portuguese (*language*)
poseer (y) to possess
posesión *f.* possession
posesivo/a possessive (7B)
posgrado/a graduate; **estudios de posgrado** graduate studies (9B)
posibilidad *f.* possibility
posible possible
posición *f.* position
positivo/a positive
postre *m.* dessert (3B)
potable: agua (*f.* [*but* el agua]) **potable** drinking water
práctica *n.* practice
practicar (qu) to practice (1A); **practicar el alpinismo de rocas** to rock climb

(6B); **practicar la escalada** to rappel; **practicar el paracaidismo** to skydive (6B); **practicar el parapente** to hang glide; **practicar el yoga** to do yoga (4A); **practicar un deporte** to practice a sport (1A)

pragmático/a pragmatic

precavido/a cautious (5A)

precio (fijo) (fixed) price (2B); **estar** (*irreg.*) **a buen precio** to be a good price

precioso/a precious; valuable; **metales** (*m.*) **preciosos** precious metals (8A)

preciso/a precise (1B); **es preciso** it's necessary (8B)

precolombino/a pre-Columbian (before Columbus)

predeterminado/a predetermined

predicción *f.* prediction

predominar to dominate

preferencia preference

preferir (ie, i) to prefer (2A)

pregunta *n.* question

preguntar to ask (questions)

preliminar preliminary

premio award; prize

prenda article of clothing (2B)

prender (las luces) to turn on (the lights)

prensa *n.* press (8B)

preocupación *f.* worry (8B); concern (8B)

preocupado/a worried (7A)

preocuparse (por) to worry (about) (7A)

preparar to prepare (1A)

preparativo preparation

preparatoria high school

preposición *f.* preposition

presencia presence

presentación *f.* presentation; introduction (P)

presentador(a) anchorman, anchorwoman (8B)

presentar to present; to introduce; to show (*a film*)

presente *n. m., adj. m. f.* present (*time*)

preservar to preserve, maintain

presidencia presidency

presidencial presidential

presidente/a president

presión *f.* pressure; **presión arterial** blood pressure (7A)

presenciar to witness

prestado/a borrowed; **pedir (i, i) prestado/a** to borrow (8A)

préstamo *n.* loan (8A); **sacar (qu) un préstamo** to take out a loan

prestar to loan, lend (8A)

presumido/a conceited (9A)

presupuesto (mensual) (monthly) budget (8A)

pretérito *gram.* preterite (tense)

pretexto pretext, excuse

prevalente prevalent

preventivo/a: señales (*f. pl.*) **preventivas** warning signs

previo/a previous

primaria: (escuela) primaria elementary school; **maestro/a de primaria** elementary school teacher (9B)

primavera spring (*season*) (1B)

primer, primero/a first; **por primera vez** for the first time; **primer (segundo, tercer) plato** first (second, third) course (6A); **primera clase** first class (6A)

primo/a cousin (3A); *pl.* cousins

principal *adj.* main, principal

principio beginning

prisa: tener (*irreg.*) **prisa** to be in a hurry

privacidad *f.* privacy

privado/a private; **casa privada** private residence (4B); **con baño privado** with a private bath (6A)

privilegiado/a privileged

probabilidad *f.* probability

probable probable; **es probable** it's probable (8B)

probador *m.* dressing room (2B)

probar (ue) to try on; **¿puedo probarme... ?** may I try on . . . ? (2B); **probarse** to try on (2B)

problema *m.* problem

problemático/a problematic

procesar to process

proceso process

producción *f.* production

producir *irreg.* to produce

producto product; **producto biodegradable** biodegradable product (6B); **producto de limpieza** cleaning product (4B); **producto desechable** disposable product (6B); **producto farmacéutico** pharmaceutical product (8A); **producto lácteo** dairy product (3B); **producto nacional bruto** gross national product; **productos de exportación** export products (8A)

productor(a) producer (9B)

profesión *f.* profession (9B)

profesional *adj.* professional

profesor(a) professor (P)

profundo/a deep

programa *m.* program; **programa de entrevistas** talk show (8B); **programa deportivo** sports show (8B); **programa televisivo** television program (8B)

programación *f.* programming

programador(a) (computer) programmer (9B)

prohibir (prohíbo) to prohibit (8B)

prólogo prologue

promedio *n.* average

promesa promise; **cumplir las promesas** to keep one's word (9A)

prometer to promise (9B)

promiscuo/a promiscuous

pronombre *m.* pronoun

pronóstico del tiempo weather report (8B)

pronto soon; **tan pronto como** as soon as (9B)

pronunciación *f.* pronunciation

pronunciar to pronounce

propiedad *f.* property

propina tip (6A); **dejar (una) propina** to leave a tip (6A)

propio/a own

proporcionar to give

propósito purpose; aim; intention; **a propósito** by the way

prosperidad *f.* prosperity (8A)

próspero/a prosperous

protección *f.* protection

proteger (j) to protect (6B)

proteína protein

protestar to protest (8B)

provecho: buen provecho enjoy your meal

provincia province, region

provocar (qu) to provoke

proximidad *f.* proximity

próximo/a next (1B)

prueba *n.* quiz, test

psicología psychology (P)

psicólogo/a psychologist (9B)

psiquiatra *m., f.* psychiatrist (9B)

publicación *f.* publication

publicar (qu) to publish

publicitario/a: anuncio publicitario commercial (8B)

público *n.* public; audience; **teléfono público** public telephone (P)

publico/a *adj.* public

pueblo small town

puerro leek

puerta door (P)

puerto (sea)port

puertorriqueño/a *n., adj.* Puerto Rican

pues... well . . .

puesto *n.* stand; **puesto que** given that

pulir to polish (4B)

pulmón *m.* lung (7A)

pulsar to click

punta de lanza spearhead

punto point; period; **en punto** on the dot (*time*) (1A); **punto de vista** point of view

puntual punctual; **ser** (*irreg.*) **puntual** to be punctual (1A)

puntualidad *f.* punctuality

puré (*m.*) **de papas** mashed potatoes (3B)

púrpura purple

Q

que that, which; than; **creer que** to think that (1B); **hasta que** *conj.* until; **lo que** what, that which (1B); **más** + *adj.* + **que** more + *adj.* + than; **tener** (*irreg.*) **que** + *inf.* to have to (*do something*)

¿qué? what? (1B); **¿a qué hora... ?** at what time... ?, when... ? (1A); **¿por qué?** why? (1B); **¿qué carrera haces?** what's your (*fam. s.*) major? (P); **¿qué clases tienes este semestre/trimestre?** what classes do you (*fam. s.*) have this semester/quarter? (P); **¿qué día es hoy?** what day is today? (1A); **¿qué estudias?** what are you (*fam. s.*) studying? (P); **¿qué hora es?** what time is it? (1A); **¿qué número calza?** what size shoe do you (*form. s.*) wear? (2B); **¿qué trae... ?** what comes with... ? (6A)

quechua *m.* Quechua (*language*)

quedar to be located (2A); **creo que le queda un poco grande** I think it's a bit big on you (2B); **¿me queda bien?** does it fit me? (2B); **quedarle bien/mal** to fit well/ poorly; **quedarse** to stay (*in a place*) (6A)

quehacer *m.* chore; **quehaceres domésticos** household chores (4B)

queja complaint

quejarse (de) to complain (about)

quemar to burn; **quemar calorías** to burn calories (4A)

querer *irreg.* to want (2A); to love (7B); **quiere decir** it means

queso cheese (3B); **queso de crema** cream cheese (3B)

quien(es) who, whom

¿quién(es)? who? whom? (1B)

química chemistry (P)

químico / mujer (*f.*) química chemist (9B)

quince fifteen (1A)

quinientos/as five hundred (2B)

quinientos mil five hundred thousand (5B)

quiosco kiosk

quitar to remove, take away; **quitar el polvo** to dust (4B); **quitarse** to take off (*clothing*)

quizá(s) perhaps

R

rabia rage; **darle** (*irreg.*) **rabia (a alguien)** to make (someone) angry

racismo racism

radio *f.* radio (*medium*)

rafting: hacer (*irreg.*) **rafting** to go rafting (6B)

raíz *f.* (*pl.* **raíces**) root; **bienes** (*m. pl.*) **raíces** real estate (8A)

ramo bouquet

rápido *adv.* fast

rápido/a *adj.* fast, quick; **comida rápida** fast food (3B)

raro/a strange; rare; **raras veces** infrequently, rarely

rascacielos *m. s.* skyscraper (2A)

rasgar (gu) to tear, rip

rasgo feature, trait (3A)

rasguñar to scratch (9A)

rato *n.* while, short time; **ratos libres** free time (4A)

ratón *m.* mouse (*animal*) (9A); mouse (*computer*) (5A)

raya stripe; **de rayas** striped (2B); **mantenerse** (*like* **tener**) **a raya** to keep (*something*) away

rayo ray; **rayos X** X-rays (7A)

raza race (*people*)

razón *f.* reason

razonable reasonable

reacción *f.* reaction

reaccionar to react (7A)

real real; royal

realidad *f.* reality

realista *adj. m., f.* realistic

reality *m.* reality show (*TV*) (8B)

realizar (c) to attain, achieve (9B)

realmente really

rebaja sale (2B)

rebelde rebellious

recargable rechargeable; **pila recargable** rechargeable battery

recargar (gu) to recharge

recepción *f.* reception

recesión *f.* recession (8A)

receta recipe; prescription (7A)

recibir to receive (1B)

recibo receipt (8A)

reciclaje *m.* recycling (6B)

reciclar to recycle (6B)

recién recently; **recién nacido/a** newborn baby (5B)

reciente recent

recipiente *m.* container

recíproco/a reciprocal

recitar to recite

recoger (j) to pick up

recomendable recommendable

recomendación *f.* recommendation

recomendar (ie) to recommend (8B)

reconocer (zc) to recognize (3A)

reconocido/a renowned

recordar (ue) to remember (2A)

recorrido trip, journey

recorte *m.* clipping (*of a magazine*)

recreación *f.* recreation

recreo recess (5A)

recuerdo memory; souvenir; **comprar recuerdos** to buy souvenirs (6B)

recuperación *f.* recuperation (8A)

recuperarse to recuperate

recurrir a to turn to

recurso resource; **recursos naturales** natural resources (6B)

red *f.* net; Internet; **navegar (gu) la red** to surf the Web (1A)

redacción *f.* composition

reducir *irreg.* to reduce

reembolso reimbursement

reemplazar (c) to replace

reenviar (reenvío) to forward

referencia reference

referir(se) (ie, i) (a) to refer (to)

refinado/a refined

reflejar to reflect

reflexivo/a reflexive

refresco soft drink (3B); **refresco dietético** diet soft drink (3B)

refrigerador *m.* refrigerator (4B)

regalar to give (*as a gift*) (3B)

regalo gift (4A)

regatear to bargain (2B)

regateo bargaining

regimen *m.* diet

región *f.* region

regresar to return (*to a place*); **regresar a casa** to go home (1A)

regulador(a) regulator

regular to regulate

reinado *n.* reign

reírse (i, i) to laugh (7A)

relación *f.* relationship

relacionado/a (con) related (to)

relacionarse to relate, be related to

relajado/a relaxed (7A)

relajante *adj.* relaxing

relajarse to relax

relatar to relate, tell

relato tale, story

religión *f.* religion

religioso/a religious

rellenar to fill

relleno/a (de) stuffed (with)

reloj *m.* clock (P); watch (P)

remar to row; **remar en canoa** to go canoeing (6B)

remedio remedy

remolino pinwheel

Renacimiento Renaissance

rencor *m.* anger; **guardar(le) rencor (a alguien)** to hold a grudge (against someone) (7B)

renovar (ue) to renew

renta per cápita per capita income

renunciar a to quit (*a job*); to give up (9A)

repartir to distribute

repasar to review (1A)

repaso review

repente: de repente suddenly

repetir (i, i) to repeat (2B)

repleto/a overflowing

reportaje *m.* report (8B)
reportar to report
reportero/a reporter (8B)
represa dam
representante *m., f.* representative (9B)
representar to represent
represivo/a repressive
reproductor (*m.*) **de CD/DVD/vídeo**
CD/DVD/video player (5A)
república republic; **República**
Dominicana Dominican Republic
requerir (ie, i) to require
requisito requirement
res *f.:* **carne** (*f.*) **de res** beef (3B)
resaltar to highlight
resentido/a resentful
reserva reserve; reservation (*hotel*)
reservación *f.* reservation (6A)
reservado/a reserved (1B)
resfriado *n.* cold (*sickness*); **tener** (*irreg.*)
un resfriado to have a cold (7A)
resfriarse (me resfrío) to catch a cold
residencia estudiantil residence hall,
dormitory (P)
resolución *f.* resolution
resolver (ue) (*p.p.* **resuelto/a**) (**conflictos**)
to resolve (conflicts) (9A)
respectivo/a respective
respetar to respect (7B); **respetar el**
espacio personal to respect personal
space (9A)
respeto respect (7B)
respetuoso/a respectful
respirar to breathe (7A)
responder to respond, answer
responsabilidad *f.* responsibility;
responsabilidad cívica civic duty (8B)
responsable responsible (8A)
respuesta response, answer
restaurante *m.* restaurant (2A); **cenar en**
un restaurante elegante to eat in a
fancy restaurant (6B)
resto rest, remainder; *pl.* remains;
remnants
restricción *f.* restriction
resuelto/a (*p.p. of* **resolver**) resolved (7B)
resultado result
resultar to turn out, result
resumen *m.* summary
resumir to sum up
retirar to withdraw
retrasar to delay, retard
retroproyectora projector
reunión *f.* (**cívica**) (town) meeting (8B)
reunirse (me reúno) to get together
revelar to reveal
revisar to check, inspect
revista magazine (1B)
revolución *f.* revolution (5B)
revuelto/a (*p.p. of* **revolver**): **huevos**
revueltos scrambled eggs (3B)

rey *m.* king; **Día** (*m.*) **de los Reyes**
Magos Epiphany (January 6), Day of
the Magi
rico/a rich, wealthy (2B); delicious (2B)
ridículo/a ridiculous (8B)
rincón *m.* corner
riñón *m.* kidney
río river (6B)
ríoplatense *adj.* pertaining to the **río de**
la plata (*Platte River*)
riqueza *s.* riches, wealth (8A)
ritmo rhythm
rito rite; ceremony
rivalidad *f.* rivalry
rizado/a curly (3A); **pelo rizado** curly
hair (3A)
robar to rob, steal
robo break-in
roca rock; **practicar** (**qu**) **el alpinismo de**
rocas to rock climb (6B)
rodear to surround
rodilla knee (7A)
rogar (ue) (gu) to beg
rojo/a red (2B)
románico/a *adj.* Romance (*language*)
romántico/a romantic (7B)
romper (*p.p.* **roto/a**) to break; **romper con**
to break up with (7B); **romperse** to
break (a bone) (7A)
roncar (qu) to snore
ronda *n.* round
ropa clothing (2B)
rosado/a pink (2B)
rosario rosary
rosbif *m.* roast beef (3B)
rosquilla bagel (3B)
rostro *n.* face
roto/a (*p.p. of* **romper**) broken
rozarse (c) con la gente to mingle with
people (4A)
rubí *m.* ruby
rubio/a blond(e) (3A); **pelo rubio** blond
hair (3A)
rueda wheel; **rueda de andar** treadmill
(4A); **rueda pinchada** flat tire
ruido noise
rumor *m.* rumor
ruso/a *n., adj.* Russian
ruta route

S

sábado Saturday (1A)
saber *irreg.* to know (*facts, information*)
(3A); to find out (*about something*);
saber + *inf.* to know how to (*do*
something) (3A); **todavía no sé** I still
don't know (P)
sabio/a wise (1B)
sabor *m.* taste, flavor

sabroso/a savory, tasty
sacar (qu) to take out; **sacar a pasear** to
take for a walk (9A); **sacar dinero** to
withdraw money (8A); **sacar fotos** to
take pictures; **sacar la basura** to take
out the trash (4B); **sacar la lengua** to
stick out one's tongue (7A); **sacar la**
licencia de conducir to get a driver's
license (5A); **sacar un préstamo** to
take out a loan; **sacar un vídeo/DVD** to
rent a video/DVD (4A); **sacarle sangre**
to draw blood (7A)
sacerdote *m.* priest
sacrificarse (qu) to sacrifice oneself (9A)
safari *m.* safari
sal *f.* salt
sala family room (4B); **sala de clase**
classroom (P); **sala de espera** waiting
room
salado/a salty (3B); **galleta salada**
cracker (3B)
salchicha sausage (3B)
salida exit; way out
salir *irreg.* to leave; to go out (2A); **¿a**
cuánto sale? how much is it?; **salir a**
bailar to go dancing; **salir con** to go
out with (7B)
salsa salsa (3B)
saltar to jump (9A); **saltar la cuerda** to
jump rope
salto: hacer (*irreg.*) **el salto bungee** to
bungee jump (6B)
salud *f.* health (7A)
saludable healthy
saludar to greet (7B)
saludo greeting
salvar to save (6B)
san *apocopated form of* **santo**
sandalia sandal (2B)
sándwich *m.* sandwich (3B)
sangre *f.* blood; **sacarle (qu) sangre** to
draw blood (7A)
sanguíneo/a *adj.* blood
santería *religion of African origin*
practiced in the Caribbean
santo/a *n., adj.* saint
se *refl. pron.* herself, himself, itself,
yourself (*form. s.*), themselves,
yourselves (*form. pl.*)
se alquila for rent (4B)
secadora dryer (4B)
sección *f.* section
seco/a dry
secreto *n.* secret; **ocultar(le) secretos**
(a alguien) to hide secrets (from
someone) (7B)
secundario/a secondary; **escuela**
secundaria high school; **maestro/a de**
secundaria high school teacher (9B)
seda silk (2B)
sedentario/a sedentary

sediento/a thirsty
seducir (zc) to seduce (7B)
seductor(a) seductive (7B)
seguida: en seguida right away
seguir (i, i) (g) to follow (2B); **seguir derecho** to continue straight ahead (6A)
según according to
segundo/a *adj.* second; **segundo plato** second course (6A)
seguramente surely
seguridad *f.* safety; **pasar por seguridad** to go through security (6A)
seguro insurance; **seguro antirrobo** antitheft insurance (8A); **seguro contra incendios** fire insurance (8A); **seguro de automóvil** automobile insurance (8A); **seguro de vida** life insurance (8A); **seguro de vivienda** homeowner's insurance (8A); **seguro médico** medical insurance (8A)
seguro/a *adj.* sure; safe; **estar (***irreg.***) seguro/a de** to be sure of (8B)
seis six (1A)
seiscientos/as six hundred (2B)
seiscientos mil six hundred thousand (5B)
selección *f.* selection; national team (*soccer*)
seleccionar to select, choose
sello seal, stamp
selva (tropical) (tropical) jungle (6B)
semáforo signal; traffic light
semana week (1A); **fin (***m.***) de semana** weekend (1A); **semana entrante** next week (1B); **semana pasada** last week
semanal weekly
semejante similar
semejanza similarity
semestre *m.* semester
semilla seed
senador(a) senator (9B)
sencillo/a simple (1B); **cama sencilla** twin (single) bed (4B)
sendero path
seno breast (*of a person*)
sensación *f.* sensation
sensacionalista *m., f.* sensationalist (8B)
sensible sensitive (7B)
sentarse (ie) to sit down
sentido *n.* sense; **sentido de dirección** sense of direction; **sentido del humor** sense of humor
sentimental sentimental (7B)
sentimiento feeling, emotion (7B)
sentir (ie, i) to feel (4B); **sentirse** to feel (*emotion, health*) (5A); **sentirse + *adj., adv*** to feel + *adj., adv.*
señal *f.* sign; signal; **señales preventivas** warning signs
señalar to point out
señor (Sr.) man; Mr.

señora (Sra.) woman; Mrs.
señorita (Srta.) young woman; Miss, Ms.
separación *f.* separation
separado/a separated (3A)
septentrional northern
septiembre September (1B)
ser *irreg.* to be (P); **¿cómo es?** what is he/she/it/like? what are you (*form. s.*) like? (3A); **¿cuál es su apellido?** what's his/her last name? (P); **¿cuál es tu apellido?** what's your (*fam. s.*) last name? (P); **¿de dónde eres?** where are you (*fam. s.*) from (P); **era** he/she/it was, you (*form. s.*) were (1B); **es buena idea** (2B); **es de...** it's made of . . . (2B); **es imposible** it's impossible (8B); **es la una** it's one o'clock (1A); **es necesario** it's necessary (2B); **es preciso** it's necessary (8B); **es probable** it's probable (8B); **mi apellido es...** my last name is . . . (P); **mi nombre es...** my name is . . . (P); **parece ser** it seems to be; he/she seems . . . (1B); **pasar a ser** to become; **¿qué hora es?** what time is it? (1A); **ser aficionado/a** to be a fan (4A); **(no) ser de fiar** to be (un)reliable (9A); **ser hábil para (las matemáticas, las ciencias)** to be good at (math, science) (9B); **ser parcial** to be biased (8A); **ser pelotero/a** to be a kiss-up (9A); **ser puntual** to be punctual (1A); **son de...** they're made of . . . (2B); **soy de...** I'm from . . . (P)
serie *f.* series
serio/a serious (1B)
serpiente *f.* snake (9A)
servicio service; **servicio de cuarto** room service (6A); **servicios médicos** medical services (9B); **servicios sociales** social services (9B)
servilleta napkin (6A)
servir (i, i) to serve (2B); **¿en qué puedo servirle?** how may I help you? (2B); **servir de compañía** to give, keep company (9A)
sesenta sixty (2A)
sesión *f.* session
setecientos/as seven hundred (2B)
setecientos mil seven hundred thousand (5B)
setenta seventy (2A)
sexo sex
si if (1B)
sí yes; **sí, por supuesto** yes, of course
SIDA (síndrome [*m.***] de inmunodeficiencia adquirida)** AIDS (Acquired Immune Deficiency Syndrome) (8B)
siempre always (3B)
siesta nap; **echar una siesta** to take a nap

siete seven (1A)
siglo century (5B); **siglo XXI** twenty-first century (5B)
significado meaning
significar (qu) to mean
significativamente significantly
signo *n.* sign (*horoscope*)
siguiente following; next
silencioso/a silent, quiet
silla chair (P)
sillón *m.* armchair (4B)
simbolizar (c) to symbolize
símbolo symbol
simbología symbology
similitud *f.* similarity
simpático/a friendly, nice (1B)
sin without (4B); **sin duda** without a doubt; **sin embargo** *conj.* however; **sin que** without (7B)
sincero/a sincere (9B)
sincretismo syncretism, consolidation of different religious doctrines
síndrome *m.* syndrome; **síndrome de inmunodeficiencia adquirida (SIDA)** Acquired Immune Deficiency Syndrome (AIDS) (8B)
sino but (rather)
sinónimo synonym
sinopsis *f.* synopsis
síntoma *m.* symptom
sinuoso/a winding
siquiera: ni siquiera not even
sistema *m.* system; **analista (***m., f.***) de sistemas** systems analyst (9B)
sitio place, location; site; **diseñador(a) de sitios** Web site designer (9B)
situación *f.* situation
situado/a situated, located
sobras *pl.* leftovers (3B)
sobre about; on, on top of (4B)
sobresaliente excellent
sobrino/a nephew, niece (3A)
sociable sociable (9A)
social social; **ciencias sociales** social sciences (P); **servicios sociales** social services (9B); **trabajador(a) social** social worker (9B)
sociedad *f.* society (8B)
socio/a associate; partner
socioeconómico/a socioeconomic
sociolingüístico/a sociolinguistic
sociología sociology (P)
sofá *m.* sofa (4B)
sofisticado/a sophisticated
soja soy(bean) (3B)
sol *m.* sun; **hace sol** it's sunny (1B); **tomar el sol** to sunbathe (1B)
solamente only (1A)
solas: a solas alone (1B)
soldado, mujer (*f.***) soldado** soldier (9B)

soler (ue) + *inf.* to be in the habit of / be accustomed to (*doing something*) (2A)
sólido/a solid
solitario/a solitary
sólo (solamente) *adv.* only; **sólo estoy mirando** I'm just looking (2B)
solo/a alone
soltero/a single, unmarried (3A); **madre** (*f.*) **soltera** single mother (3A); **padre** (*m.*) **soltero** single father (3A)
solución *f.* solution
solucionar to solve
sombrero hat
sonar (ue) to ring
soneto sonnet
sonreír (i, i) to smile
sonrisa smile
sonrojarse to blush (7B)
soñador(a) dreamer (1B)
soñar (ue) (con) to dream (about) (5A)
sopa soup (3B)
soplo breeze; breath
soporte *m.* support
sorprendente surprising
sorprender to surprise
sorpresa surprise; **fiesta de sorpresa** surprise party (4A)
sospechar to suspect
sospechoso/a suspicious (1B)
sostener (*like* **tener**) to hold up, support
sótano basement
su(s) *poss.* his, her, its, their, your (*form. s., pl.*) (1A); **¿cuál es su apellido?** what's his/her last name? (P)
subdivisión *f.* subdivision; subsection
subida rise (8A)
subir to rise, go up (8A); **subir a** to board (6A); **subirse a los árboles** to climb trees (5A)
subjuntivo *gram.* subjunctive (mood)
sublevarse to revolt
subrayar to underline
suburbio suburb
suceder to happen
sucesión *f.* succession
suceso event, happening
sucio/a dirty
sudadera sweatshirt (2B)
Sudamérica South America (6B)
sudamericano/a *n., adj.* South American
sudar to sweat (4A)
suegro/a father-in-law, mother-in-law (3A)
sueldo (mínimo) (minimum) wage, salary (8A)
suelo floor
sueño *n.* dream; **tener** (*irreg.*) **sueño** to be sleepy (7A)
suerte *f.* luck; **tener** (*irreg.*) **suerte** to be lucky
suéter *m.* sweater (2B)

suficiente sufficient, enough
sufrir to suffer
sugerencia suggestion
sugerir (ie, i) to suggest (4B)
suicidio suicide
sujeto *n.* subject
sumar to add
superar to exceed
supermercado supermarket (2A)
supuesto/a (*p.p. of* **suponer**) supposed; **por supuesto** of course
sur *m.* south; **al sur de** to the south of (2A)
surfear to surf (6B)
suroeste *m.* southwest
suspender to suspend
sustancia substance
sustancial substantial
sustantivo noun
sustentable: desarrollo sustentable sustainable development
sustitución *f.* substitution
sustituir (y) to substitute
suyo/a/os/as *poss.* your, of yours (*form. s., pl.*); his, of his; her, of hers (2B)

T

tabaco tobacco (8A)
tacaño/a greedy, stingy (7B)
tacón *m.* heel (*shoe*); **zapatos de tacón alto** high-heeled shoes (2B)
tal such, such a; **con tal de que** *conj.* provided that (7B); **¿qué tal?** how's it going?; **tal vez** perhaps
talento talent
talentoso/a talented
talla size (*clothes*) (2B); **¿cuál es su talla?** what size do you (*form. s.*) wear? (2B)
tamaño size (4B); **¿de qué tamaño es... ?** what size is . . . ? (4B)
también also, too (1A)
tampoco neither, not either (3B)
tan so; **tan... como** as . . . as (3A); **tan pronto como** as soon as (9B)
tanto *adv.* so much
tanto/a *adj.* so much; such; *pl.* so many; **tanto/a/os/as... como** as much/many . . . as (3A)
tapada: tener (*irreg.*) **la nariz tapada** to have a stuffed-up nose
tarántula tarantula (9A)
tardar to take time (*to do something*)
tarde *n. f.* afternoon, evening; **buenas tardes** good afternoon/evening (P); **de la tarde** in the afternoon, evening (P.M.) (1A); **por la tarde** in the afternoon/evening (1A)
tarde *adv.* late (1A)
tarea homework (2A); task
tarifa rate, price, fare

tarjeta card (4A); **tarjeta de crédito** credit card (2B); **tarjeta de felicitación** greeting card
tasa rate, level; **tasa de desempleo** unemployment rate (8A)
taxista *m., f.* taxi driver
taza cup (*coffee*) (6A)
tazón *m.* bowl
te *d.o.* you (*fam. s.*); *i.o.* to/for you (*fam. s.*); *refl. pron.* yourself (*fam. s.*); **¿cómo te llamas?** what is your (*fam. s.*) name? (P); **te gusta...** you (*fam. s.*) like . . . (1A)
té (*m.*) **(caliente/helado)** (hot/iced) tea (3B)
teatro theater
teclado keyboard (5A)
técnica technique
técnico/a *n.* technician (9B); *adj.* technical
tecnología technology
tecnológico/a technological
tejido/a woven
telefónica telephone company
teléfono telephone; **llamar por teléfono** to call on the telephone (1A); **teléfono celular** cell phone (5A); **teléfono público** public telephone (P)
telenovela soap opera (8B)
telepático/a telepathic
televidente *m., f.* television viewer
televisión *f.* television (*medium*); **canal** (*m.*) **de televisión** television channel; **ver** (*irreg.*) **la televisión** to watch TV
televisivo/a *adj.* television; **programa** (*m.*) **televisivo** television program (8B)
televisor *m.* television (*set*) (P)
tema *m.* theme, topic
temer to fear
temperatura temperature; **tomar(le) la temperatura** to take (*someone's*) temperature (7A)
temporada season (*sports*)
temprano early (1A)
tendencia tendency
tender (ie) to tend to
tenedor *m.* fork (6A)
tener *irreg.* to have (2A); **tener... años** to be . . . years old (2A); **tener celos** to be jealous; **tener don de gentes** to have a way with people (9B); **tener éxito** to be successful (5B); **tener expectativas** to have expectations; **tener fiebre** to have a fever (7A); **tener ganas de** + *inf.* to feel like (*doing something*); **tener hambre** to be hungry; **tener la nariz tapada** to have a stuffed-up nose (7A); **tener prisa** to be in a hurry; **tener que** + *inf.* to have to (*do something*); **tener sueño** to be sleepy (7A); **tener suerte** to be lucky; **tener un resfriado** to have a cold (7A); **tenerle cariño a alguien** to be fond of someone (7B); **tenerle**

envidia (a alguien) to be envious (of someone) (7A); **tenerle miedo (a alguien)** to be afraid (of someone) (7A); **tengo una clase de…** I have a(n) … class (P); **¿tiene Ud. la hora?** do you (*form. s.*) have the time? (1A)

tenis *m.* tennis (4A); **cancha de tenis** tennis court (4A); **zapatos de tenis** tennis shoes (2B)

tensión *f.* tension; **tensión arterial** blood pressure

tenso/a tense (7A); stressed

tentación *f.* temptation

terapeuta *m., f.* therapist (9B)

tercer, tercero/a third; **tercer plato** third course (6A)

terco/a stubborn

terminación *f.* ending

terminar to finish (7B)

término term

termostato thermostat

terraza terrace

terremoto earthquake (5B)

terrenos *pl.* lands

terrestre terrestrial

territorio territory

terrorismo terrorism (8B)

terrorista *n. m., f.* terrorist

testigo *n. m., f.* witness (8B)

testimonio testimony

textiles *m., pl.* textiles (8A)

texto text; **libro de texto** textbook

ti *obj. of prep.* you (*fam. s.*) (4B)

tibio/a warm

tiburón *m.* shark

tiempo weather, time; **a tiempo** on time; **¿cuánto tiempo hace que… ?** how long has it been since … ? **hace buen/mal tiempo** it's good/bad weather (1B); **hace (mucho) tiempo** (a long time) ago; **llegar (gu) a tiempo** to arrive on time (1A); **pasar (mucho) tiempo** to spend (a lot of) time (1A); **pérdida de tiempo** waste of time (8B); **pronóstico del tiempo** weather report (8B)

tienda store, shop (2A)

tierra earth, land

tijeras *pl.* scissors

timbre *m.* bell; ring (*tone*)

tímido/a timid (1B)

tinto/a: vino tinto red wine (3B)

tío/a uncle, aunt (3A); *pl.* aunts and uncles

típico/a typical

tipo type; **tipos de interés** interest rates (8A)

tiras cómicas comics (5A); cartoons

tirar to throw out (6B)

titular *m.* headline (8B)

titularse to be titled

título title

tiza chalk (P)

toalla (de papel) (paper) towel (4B)

tocar (qu) (el piano / la guitarra) to play (the piano / the guitar) (1A); to touch

tocino bacon (3B)

todavía still, yet; **todavía no sé** I still don't know (P)

todo/a all; every; **todas las noches** every night (1A); **todos los días** every day (1A)

tolerante tolerant (9A)

tomar to take (1A); to drink (1A); **tomar apuntes** to take notes (1A); **tomar café** to drink coffee (1A); **tomar cerveza** to drink beer (1A); **tomar el sol** to sunbathe (1B); **tomar una clase** to take a class (1A); **tomar(le) la temperatura** to take (*someone's*) temperature (7A); **tomarse algo muy a pecho** to take something to heart (7A); to feel something intensely (7A)

tomate *m.* tomato (3B)

tono tone

tontería foolish thing

tonto/a silly, foolish (1B)

topacio topaz

torbellino whirlwind

tormentoso/a stormy

toronja grapefruit (3B)

torpe clumsy (5A)

torre *f.* tower (2A)

torta cake

tortilla (de maíz) *thin cake made of cornmeal or flour* (3B); **tortilla española** *omelette made of eggs, potatoes, and onions* (*Sp.*) (3B)

tortuga turtle (9A)

tos *f.* cough; **jarabe** (*m.*) **para la tos** cough syrup

tostada de pan a la francesa French toast (3B)

tostado/a toasted; **pan** (*m.*) **tostado** toast (3B)

trabajador(a) *adj.* hardworking (1B); *n.* worker; **trabajador(a) social** social worker (9B)

trabajar to work (1A); **trabajar en equipo** to work as a team (9A)

trabajo job; **Día** (*m.*) **del Trabajo** Labor Day

trabársele la lengua a alguien to get tongue-tied (7B)

tradicional traditional; **pérdida de valores tradicionales** loss of traditional values (8B)

traducir (*like* **conducir**) to translate

traer *irreg.* to bring (2A); **¿me podría traer… ?** could you (*form. s.*) bring me … ? **¿qué trae… ?** what comes with … ? (6A)

tráfico traffic

tragedia tragedy

traicionar to betray (7B)

traje *m.* suit (2B); **traje de baño** bathing suit (2B)

trama plot (*of a story*)

tranquilo/a calm, peaceful

transacción *f.* transaction

transición *f.* transition

tránsito traffic

transmitir to transmit

transparente transparent

transporte *m.* transportation (6A)

trapo rag (4B)

tras *adv.* behind

tratado treaty; **Tratado de Libre Comercio (TLC)** North America Free Trade Agreement (NAFTA)

tratamiento treatment

tratar to treat; to deal with; **tratarse de** to be about (8A)

través: a través de through, by means of

travieso/a mischievous (5A)

trece thirteen (1A)

treinta thirty (1A); **los años treinta** the thirties (2A)

treinta y dos thirty-two (2A)

treinta y uno thirty-one (2A)

tren *m.* train; **estación** (*f.*) **del tren** train station (2B)

tres three (1A)

tres mil three thousand (5B)

trescientos/as three hundred (2B)

trescientos mil three hundred thousand (5B)

trimestre *m.* quarter (*school*)

triste sad (1B)

triunfo triumph (9B)

tropical: selva tropical tropical jungle (6B)

trotar to jog (4A)

trozo piece, chunk

truco trick; **hacer** (*irreg.*) **trucos** to do tricks (9A)

tú *sub. pron.* you (*fam. s.*) (P)

tu(s) *poss.* your (*fam. s.*) (1A); **¿cuál es tu apellido?** what's your (*fam. s.*) last name? (P)

tumultuoso/a tumultuous (5B)

turista *n. m., f.* tourist

turístico/a *adj.* tourist; **clase** (*f.*) **turística** tourist class (6A)

tutearse to address each other as **tú**

tuyo/a/os/as *poss.* your, of yours (*fam. s.*) (2B)

U

u or (*used instead of* **o** *before words beginning with* **o** *or* **ho**)

ubicación *f.* location

ubicado/a located

último/a last

umbral (*m.*) **de la pobreza** poverty line

un, uno/a *indef. art.* a, an; one (P); *pl.* some, any; **a la una** at one o'clock (1A); **es la una** it's one o'clock (1A); **un poco de** a little (of) (P); **una vez al mes** once a month (1B)

único/a only; **hijo/a único/a** only child (3A)

unión *f.* union

universidad *f.* university (P)

universitario/a *of or pertaining to the university*

uno one (1A); **cada uno** each one

urbano/a urban

uruguayo/a *n., adj.* Uruguayan

usar to use; to wear (*clothing*)

uso *n.* use

usted (Ud.) *sub. pron.* you (*form. s.*) (P); *obj. of prep.* you (*form. s.*)

ustedes (Uds.) *sub. pron.* you (*form. pl.*) (P); *obj. of prep.* you (*form. pl.*)

usuario/a user

útil useful

utilizar (c) to utilize, use

uva grape

V

vaca cow

vacación *f.* vacation; **de vacaciones** on vacation

vacío/a empty

vainilla vanilla

Valentín: Día (*m.*) **de San Valentín** St. Valentine's Day (4A)

válido/a valid

valiente brave

valle *m.* valley (6B)

valor *m.* value; **Bolsa de valores** stock market (8A); **pérdida de valores tradicionales** loss of traditional values (8B)

valorar to value

vano/a vain (9A)

vapor steam; **al vapor** steamed (3B)

vaqueros jeans (2B)

variación *f.* variation

variar (varío) to vary

variedad *f.* variety

varios/as *pl.* various

vasco: País (*m.*) **Vasco** Basque country

vaso glass (*water*) (6A)

vecindad *f.* neighborhood (4B)

vecindario neighborhood

vecino/a neighbor (4B)

vegetal *m.* vegetable

vegetariano/a vegetarian (3B)

vehículo vehicle

veinte twenty (1A); **los años veinte** the twenties (5B)

veinticinco twenty-five (1A)

veinticuatro twenty-four (1A)

veintidós twenty-two (1A)

veintinueve twenty-nine (1A)

veintiocho twenty-eight (1A)

veintiséis twenty-six (1A)

veintisiete twenty-seven (1A)

veintitrés twenty-three (1A)

veintiún, veintiuno/a twenty-one (1A)

velo veil

velocidad *f.* speed

vendaje *m.* bandage

vendedor(a) salesperson; vendor

vender to sell (2B)

vengativo/a vengeful (7A)

venir *irreg.* to come (2A)

venta sale; **de venta** for sale (4B)

ventaja advantage

ventana window (P)

ver *irreg.* (*p.p.* **visto/a**) to see (1B); **nos vemos** see you around; **ver la televisión** to watch TV; **ver un espectáculo** to see a show (6B); **ver una película** to watch a movie

verano summer (1B)

veras: de veras really

verbo verb

verdad *f.* truth

verdadero/a true

verde green (2B); unripe; **judías verdes** green beans (3B)

verdura vegetable (3B)

vergüenza shame

verificar (qu) to check, verify

verso line (of poetry)

vestido *n.* dress (2B)

vestir (i, i) to dress (2B); **vestirse** to get dressed (2B)

veterano/a veteran

veterinario/a veterinarian; **llevar al / a la veterinario/a** to take to the veterinarian (9A)

vez *f.* (*pl.* **veces**) times; **a veces** sometimes; **cada vez** each time; **cada vez más** more and more; **de vez en cuando** once in a while (3B); **la próxima vez** the next time; **la última vez** the last time; **muchas veces** often; **pagar (gu) de una vez** to pay off all at once (8A); **raras veces** infrequently, rarely; **tal vez** perhaps; **una vez (al mes)** once (a month) (1B)

vía way; path; **país** (*m.*) **en vías de desarrollo** developing country (8A)

viajar to travel, take a trip (1A)

viaje *m.* trip; **agencia de viajes** travel agency (6A); **agente** (*m., f.*) **de viajes** travel agent (6A); **hacer** (*irreg.*) **un viaje** to take a trip (6A)

viajero/a traveler (6A); **cheque** (*m.*) **de viajero** traveler's check (8A)

vida life; **seguro de vida** life insurance (8A)

vídeo video; **reproductor** (*m.*) **de vídeo** video player (5A); **sacar (qu) un vídeo** to rent a video (4A)

videocámara camcorder (5A)

videojuego video game; **jugar (ue) (gu) a los videojuegos** to play video games (5A)

vidrio glass; **botella de vidrio** glass bottle (6B)

viejo/a *n.* elderly person; **Noche** (*f.*) **Vieja** New Year's Eve (4A)

viento wind; **hace (mucho) viento** it's (very) windy (1B)

viernes *m. inv.* Friday (1A)

vigilar to watch (over); to supervise

villano/a villain; antagonist

vino wine (3); **degustar vinos** to go wine tasting (6B); **vino blanco** white wine (3B); **vino tinto** red wine (3B)

viña vineyard

violencia violence; **violencia doméstica** domestic violence (8B)

violento/a violent (8B); **crimen** (*m.*) **violento** violent crime (8B)

virtud *f.* virtue

visitar to visit (1A); **visitar a la familia** to visit one's family (1A); **visitar un museo** to visit a museum (4A)

víspera eve; day before

vista view (4A); **punto de vista** point of view

vistazo glance; **echar un vistazo** to look over

vitalicio/a for life

viudo/a widowed (3A); widower, widow

vivienda housing (4B); **seguro de vivienda** homeowner's insurance (8A)

vivir to live (1B)

vivo/a alive (3A)

vocabulario vocabulary

vocal *f.* vowel

volante *m.* steering wheel

volar (ue) to fly

volcán *m.* volcano (6B)

volcánico/a volcanic

vólibol *m.* volleyball (4A)

volumen *m.* volume; **bajar el volumen** to lower the volume; **poner** (*irreg.*) **alto el volumen** to turn the volume up high

voluntario/a volunteer (8B); **trabajar de voluntario/a** to volunteer

volver (ue) (*p.p.* **vuelto/a**) to return (*to a place*) (2A); **volver a** + *inf.* to (*do something*) again

vos *fam. s.* you (*used instead of* **tú** *in certain countries of Central and South America*)

vosotros/as *sub. pron.* you (*fam. pl. Sp.*) (P); *obj. of prep.* you (*fam. pl. Sp.*)

votante *m., f.* voter

votar to vote (8B)

voto: derecho al voto right to vote

voz *f.* (*pl.* **voces**) voice; **en voz alta** aloud

vuelo (directo) (direct) flight (6A); **asistente** (*m., f.*) **de vuelo** flight attendant (6A)

vuelta *n.* turn; **dar** (*irreg.*) **la vuelta a** to go around (*something*); **de ida y vuelta** *adj.* round-trip (6A)

vuelto/a (*p.p. of* **volver**) returned

vuestro/a/os/as *poss.* your (*fam. pl. Sp.*), of yours (*fam. pl. Sp.*) (1A)

W

web Web (World Wide Web); **página web** Web page (5A)

X

X: rayos X X-rays (7A)

Y

y and (P); **y cuarto** quarter past (*hour*) (1A); **y media** half past (*hour*) (1A)

ya already; **ya murió** he/she already died (3A); **ya no** no longer

yeso cast (*for a broken bone*)

yo *sub. pron.* I (P)

yoga *m.* yoga; **practicar (qu) el yoga** to do yoga (4A)

yogur *m.* yogurt (3B)

Z

zanahoria carrot (3A)

zapatería shoe store

zapatilla slipper (2B)

zapato shoe (2B); **zapatos de cuero** leather shoes; **zapatos de tacón alto** high-heeled shoes (2B); **zapatos de tenis** tennis shoes (2B)

zapping: **hacer** (*irreg.*) *zapping* to channel surf (5A)

zona zone

zumo juice (*Sp.*)